Jump Into Phonics

Strategies to Help Students Succeed with Phonics
Grade 2

by
Susan Ludwig

Carson-Dellosa Publishing Company, Inc.
Greensboro, North Carolina

This book has been correlated to state, national, and Canadian provincial standards. Visit *www.carsondellosa.com* to search for and view its correlations to your standards.

Layout and Cover Design: Lori Jackson

Printed in the USA • All rights reserved.   ISBN 978-1-60418-146-3

Table of Contents

Table of Contents, continued

Skills Index

CD-104291   •   Jump Into Phonics   •   © Carson-Dellosa

Introducing *Jump Into Phonics*

About This Book

Jump Into Phonics: Second Grade includes ready-to-use phonics practice activities for students who are struggling with phonics skills. This book features the skills appropriate for second-grade students and includes fun and unique activities.

Organization

Jump Into Phonics presents consonant sounds first, followed by consonant blends and digraphs, short vowels and R-controlled vowels, long vowels, vowel digraphs and diphthongs, prefixes and suffixes, contractions, syllabication, and homophones. Each teacher may choose to use this book in conjunction with the scope and sequence of his school's curriculum or base his teaching on students' individual needs.

Each unit includes a diagnostic test, teacher notes and activities, and student activities targeted to specific items on the diagnostic test, as well as review pages to assess learning. In addition, a comprehensive review test is included at the end of the book. The tests and activities are specifically designed to help teachers assess their students' needs and focus their teaching efforts.

Before incorporating student pages, pre-teaching the words will ensure every learner receives the background to study a particular letter/sound association. Some images and objects may be unfamiliar to students, creating opportunities for teachable moments to enrich your phonics instruction. Pre-teaching the words builds vocabulary, creates interest, and ensures that your phonics instruction reaches every student.

Diagnostic Tests

The diagnostic tests target the fundamental concepts of the phonics skills. These tests can be used to analyze student errors and can be modified as needed. Each test includes a teacher assessment area for easy identification of each student's strengths and weaknesses.

Teacher Notes and Teacher Activities

The teacher notes provide information about potential student problem areas. Extension and enrichment strategies, ideas for differentiation, and word lists are included for each letter/sound association.

Student Activities

Student practice activities are included for each letter/sound association. These activities provide practice, remediation, and review. The student activity pages can be easily used to differentiate instruction.

Review

Review activities help reinforce skills. Students can practice letter/sound association and complete activities that showcase their acquired knowledge.

End of Book Test

A comprehensive test at the end of this book includes the letter/sound associations for each skill covered in *Jump into Phonics: Second Grade*. This assessment can be used to summarize students' learning at the end of the year or as a benchmark test to record student progress. This comprehensive test is a valuable addition to student portfolios.

Word Cards

Word cards for each skill can be used in a variety ways. The cards can be copied and sent home for extra practice or used as an aid in instruction and guided/independent practice. Word cards can also be used with English Language Learners to introduce new vocabulary and ensure accurate comprehension of the words used throughout the book.

Diagnostic Test: Consonants

Unit I: Consonants

Directions: Say the name of each picture. Circle the letter of the beginning sound.

1.
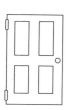

d   t

2.

t   m

3.

c   g

Directions: Say the name of each picture. Write the letter of the beginning sound.

4.
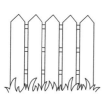

_____

5.

_____

6.

_____

Directions: Say the name of each picture. Circle the letter of the ending sound.

7.

t   g

8.

s   r

9.

l   m

Directions: Say the name of each picture. Write the letter of the ending sound.

10.
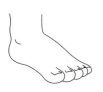

_____

11.

_____

12.

_____

Directions: Read each sentence. Write the consonants from the letter box that complete each word.

LETTER BOX		
ll	pp	tt

13.　Sally found an old book in the a _____ _____ ic.

14.　Jim was ha _____ _____ y because he did well on his math test.

15.　A mouse is sma _____ _____ er than a rat.

Directions: Read each word. If the *c* makes the /s/ sound, as in *cent*, circle the *s*. If the *c* makes the /k/ sound, as in *car*, circle the *k*.

16. mice　　　　　　s　　　　　　　k

17. cap　　　　　　s　　　　　　　k

Directions: Read each word. If the *g* makes the /g/ sound, as in *good*, circle the *g*. If the *g* makes the /j/ sound, as in *gentle*, circle the *j*.

18. girl　　　　　　g　　　　　　　j

19. gem　　　　　　g　　　　　　　j

Teacher Assessment Area

Directions: Shade the boxes that correspond to correct test items.

TOTAL CORRECT: _____

Skill	Item Number					
Initial Consonants	1	2	3	4	5	6
Final Consonants	7	8	9	10	11	12
Medial Consonants	13	14	15			
Hard/Soft c	16	17				
Hard/Soft g	18	19				

CD-104291　•　Jump Into Phonics　•　© Carson-Dellosa

Teacher Notes and Activities

Consonant Sounds

When reviewing consonant sounds, remind students of the difference between consonant sounds that are reliable and those that are not. Most initial consonants have one sound, so they are considered reliable. Included in the list of reliable initial consonant letters are *b, d, f, h, j, k, l, m, n, p, r, s, t, v, w, y,* and *z.* Although *b* and *d* are reliable letter sounds, they should be taught in isolation to avoid confusion. (Some students may have difficulty discriminating between the similar letter shapes.)

Other consonants, such as *c* and *g,* have more than one sound. These initial consonants are not considered reliable because the sounds they make vary depending on the vowel sound that follows. Introduce the letter *c* by explaining its two sounds, the /k/ sound, as in *cat,* and the /s/ sound, as in *circus.* The letter *g* is also not reliable and can represent either the /g/ sound, as in *game,* or the /j/ sound, as in *gentle.* For beginning readers, the hard sounds of these letters, /k/ and /g/, are taught first.

Many letters that are reliable as initial consonants can be silent when they appear in the middle of a word. The letters *b, d, f, g, l, m, p,* and *t* are often silent when doubled in the middle of a word. For example, only one *t* is pronounced in the word *bottom.*

As with initial consonants, many final consonants almost always have the same sound. Included in the list of reliable final consonants are *b, d, f, k, r,* and *t.* The letter *c* is not as reliable and does not usually appear at the end of one- or two-syllable words. The letter *g* usually represents the /g/ sound when it is in the final consonant position, as in *big.* The letters *h* and *j* do not usually appear as final consonants. The letter *s* is often doubled when it appears in the final position of a word, as in *dress.* The letter *v* is usually followed by a silent *e* when it appears in the final consonant position of a word, as in *give.* The letter *x* represents the /ks/ sound as the final consonant in words such as *box* and *mix.* The letter *w* does appear at the end of words, but its sound is usually part of the *ow* diphthong. The letter *y* represents a vowel sound or is part of the *oy* diphthong when it appears in the final position of a word.

Encourage students to listen to all of the sounds in a word. Teach them to stretch the sounds in the word. Tell students to tap their shoulders when making the initial sound, their elbows when making the middle sound, and their hands when making the final sound. This practice will reinforce the sounds of each word.

Display the consonant letters on an alphabet chart or class word wall. Encourage students to refer to it often for reinforcement in their reading and writing.

Unit I: Consonants

Teacher Activity 1: Same Sounds

Write each consonant on an index card. Place the index cards into a paper bag or a hat. Tell students that this game allows them to use their consonant awareness skills. Give each student a sheet of paper with a vertical line drawn through the middle. Students should write the word *Beginning* above the left column and the word *End* above the right column. Once students have their papers ready, they should draw cards from the bag, and place them facedown on their desks. Tell students that when you say, "Go," they will have five minutes to list all of the words they can that have the same beginning or ending sounds as their consonants. Students should write their words in the correct columns on their papers. After five minutes, have students count their words before sharing them with the class.

Teacher Activity 2: Consonants in Action

Students should enjoy actively searching for consonant sounds in the context of their daily reading activities. Instruct students to write all of the consonant letters on the left side of a sheet of notebook paper. Then, write all of the consonant letters on the board. Tell students to search for words in a subject-related text (e.g., a reading, social studies, or science book) that begin with each consonant. Students should record the words they find beside the corresponding consonants on their papers. When students have written a word for each consonant, have each student write one of her words next to a consonant on the board.

Teacher Activity 3: Beginning, Middle, and End Bending

Students should enjoy this kinesthetic approach to decoding words. Give each student three different colorful chenille craft sticks. Demonstrate how the chenille craft sticks can be bent to form different shapes. Allow students time to experiment with the chenille craft sticks until they can easily form different shapes. Tell students that when you say a word, they should listen for the beginning, middle, and final consonant sounds. After they identify the word's sounds, they should bend their chenille craft sticks into the shape of the consonant sounds that they heard. Use the word list (page 13) as a reference as well as any additional words that you feel will challenge students. At the end of the activity, let students form the chenille craft sticks into their favorite consonant sounds or consonant sounds that appear in their names.

Teacher Activity 4: Sound Swap

Divide the class into pairs. Give each pair a small paper plate, a small whiteboard, two write-on/wipe-away markers, an eraser, a pencil, a paper clip, and a list of three- and four-letter words. Have one student in each group draw a line across the center of the plate. On one side of the plate, students should write the word *beginning* and on the other side, students should write the word *end*. Demonstrate how they can use the tip of a pencil and a paper clip to create a spinner. Explain that one student in each group should choose a word from the list and write it on the whiteboard. His partner should spin the paper clip on the paper plate to determine if he must change the first or last letter. Students should swap letters to create new words. For example, *pat* could be changed to *hat* or *pan*. A student earns one point each time he is able to swap a letter and create a new word. The game continues as students take turns writing a new word on the whiteboard and swapping sounds. Have students share examples of the sound swaps they used to create new words.

　　CD-104291 • Jump Into Phonics • © Carson-Dellosa

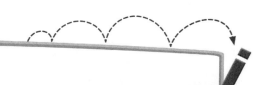

Unit I: Consonants

Teacher Activity 5: Beginning, Middle, End Rename Game

Students can create new words from the sounds they hear in another word. Tell students that you will say a word, such as *tiger*. Encourage students to listen to the sounds in that word. Then, you will say, "beginning," "middle," or "end." Depending on the word you say, students should create lists of words that begin with the consonant sound in that position. For example, if you say, "middle" for the word *tiger*, students should list words that begin with the /g/ sound. Continue the activity using different words. Have each student share one word with the class.

Teacher Activity 6: Personal Word Wall

Have students create personal word walls they can use for reference throughout the year. Give each student a manila folder. Instruct students to write each letter of the alphabet in rows or columns on their folder. Provide students with a list of challenging words to copy onto their folders. Have students draw stars beside words they feel they can use correctly. Students can add to their lists throughout the year.

Building Language

Note the following examples of words containing consonants in the initial, medial, and final positions. These sample words have been used throughout the book. Prior to teaching these letter/sound associations, familiarize students with the words to ensure that they hear each word sound and understand each word meaning.

Initial consonants: bag, bat, bell, bone, cage, can, car, cat, dice, dog, duck, fan, fire, fork, goal, gum, hand, hat, hose, hook, jet, lips, leg, log, map, mug, nail, nest, pan, pen, pin, rope, rug, tent, top, van, vest, well, yak

Medial consonants: apple, button, camel, carrot, flower, guitar, hammer, juggle, lemon, mitten, mixer, rabbit, robot, ruler, seven, slipper, shovel, spider, wallet, waffle, wagon, zipper

Final consonants: ax, bag, bed, bell, bib, book, box, car, cat, cup, fan, flag, foot, fox, goal, ham, jar, jet, leg, log, map, mop, net, pen, pig, pin, rug, shell, six, tag, ten, web, well, yak

Hard and soft *c*: cage, cake, cane, cap, car, cat, cave, celery, cent, circle, city, coat, cup

Hard and soft *g*: game, gate, gem, germ, giant, giraffe, girl, goal, goat, gold, golf, goose, guitar, gum, gym

Beginning Consonants

Directions: Say the name of each picture. Circle the letter of the beginning sound.

1.
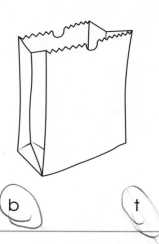

b   t

2.
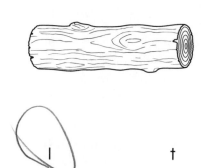

l   t

3.
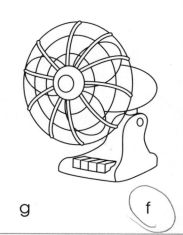

g   f

4.

c   b

5.

m   n

6.

f   d

7.

b   v

8.

b   d

9.
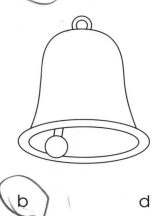

f   p

NAME: _____ **DATE:** _____

Beginning Consonants

Directions: Say the name of each picture. Write the letter of the beginning sound.

1.

___J___ et

2.

___b___ one

3.

___C___ an

4.

_____ at

5.

___F___ ire

6.

___h___ and

7.
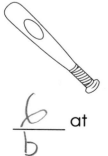
C _____ at

8.

___t___ op

9.

___T___ ent

10.

___b___ at

11.

___V___ est

12.

___f___ ork

NAME: bed _____ DATE: _____

Consonants

Beginning Consonants

Directions: Say the name of each picture. Write the letter of the beginning sound.

1.

C K age

2.

L eg

3.

M ap

4.

r ug

5.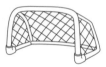

g oal

6.

l ips

7.

y ak

8.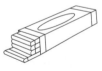

g um

9.

d uck

10.

p in

11.

n ail

12.

r ope

CD-104291 • Jump Into Phonics • © Carson-Dellosa

NAME: _____   DATE: _____

Beginning Consonants

Directions: Circle the word that names each picture. Then, write the letter of the beginning sound.

1.
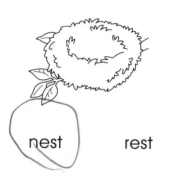
nest   rest
_____

2.
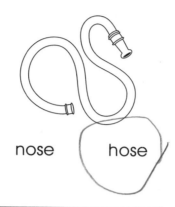
nose   hose
_____

3.
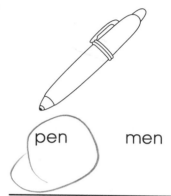
pen   men
_____

4.
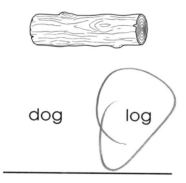
dog   log
_____

5.

book   hook
_____

6.
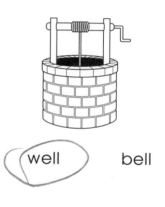
well   bell
_____

7.
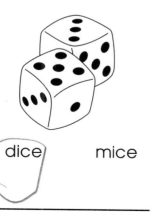
dice   mice
_____

8.
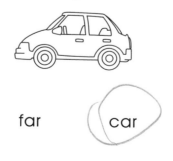
far   car
_____

9.

hat   mat
_____

Beginning Consonants

Directions: Write the word from the word box that completes each sentence.

WORD BOX

bat	bed	bib	dog
doll	field	forest	yard

1. There are many trees in a ___yard forest___ .

2. My ___dog___ barks when the doorbell rings.

3. My little sister plays with her new ___doll___ .

4. I help my mom when she rakes the ___yard___ .

5. I have a baseball ___bat___ , a ball, and a glove.

6. Mike has a brown and blue blanket on his ___bed___ .

7. My baby brother wears a ___bib___ when he eats.

8. I saw three cows standing in a ___field___ .

CD-104291 • Jump Into Phonics • © Carson-Dellosa

Ending Consonants

Consonants

Directions: Circle the word that names each picture.

1.

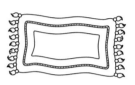

(rug)   run

2.

bat   (bag)

3.

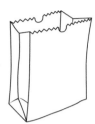

(pin)   pig

4.

(cat)   cow

5.

(yak)   yam

6.

lap   (leg)

7.

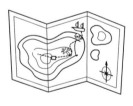

(map)   man

8.

far   (fan)

9.

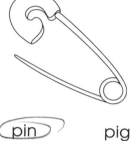

jet   (jar)

10.

sit   (six)

10.

(bed)   beg

10.

hat   (ham)

Consonants

Ending Consonants

Directions: Say the name of each picture. Write the letter of the ending sound.

1.
10

n

2.

x

3.

t

4.

g

5.

K

6.

r

Directions: Write words from the word box to complete each sentence.

WORD BOX					
ball	bib	cat	gas	jam	van

bed

7. My pet _____ cat

played with a _____ ball .

8. The baby spilled blueberry _____ Jam

on her new green _____ bib .

9. We saw a _____ van

on the street that ran out of _____ gas .

Ending Consonants

Consonants

Directions: Say the name of each picture. Draw a line from each picture to the letter of its ending sound.

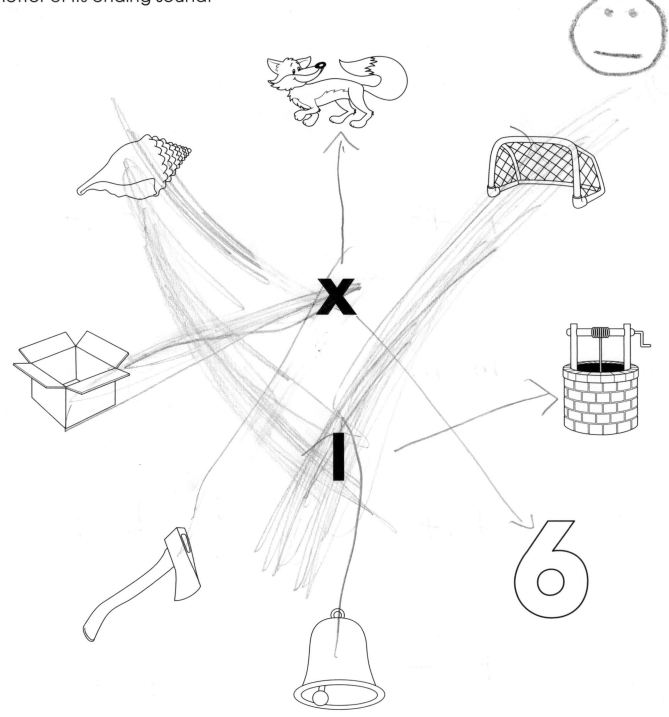

Consonants

Medial Consonants

Directions: Look at each picture and say the word. Write the letters of the middle consonant sound.

apple

1. wa _f_ _f_ les

2.  ca _r_ _r_ ot

3.  ha _m_ _m_ er

4. ju _g_ _g_ le

5. mi _t_ _t_ en

6.  ra _b_ _b_ it

7.  bu _t_ _t_ on

8. zi _p_ _p_ er

CD-104291 • Jump Into Phonics • © Carson-Dellosa

Medial Consonants

Directions: Draw a line from each word to the picture with the same middle consonant sound.

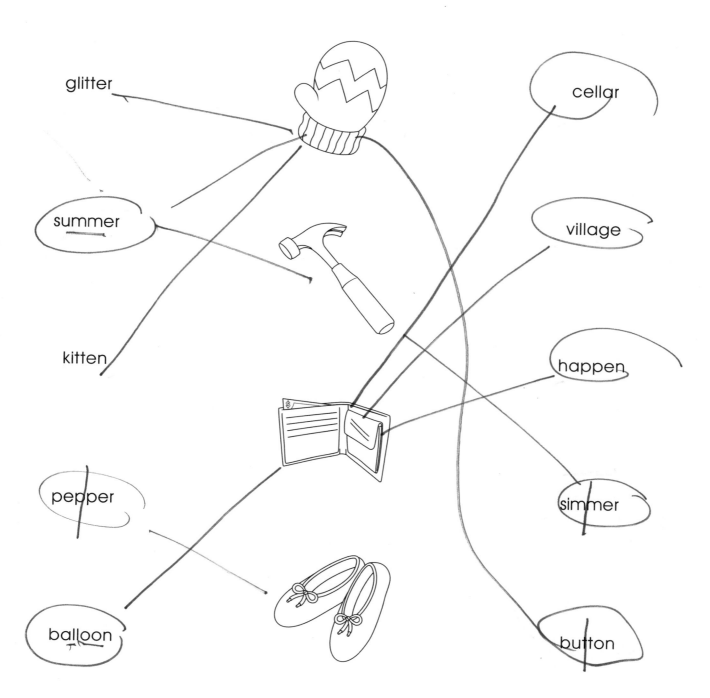

glitter

cellar

summer

village

kitten

happen

pepper

simmer

balloon

button

NAME: _____ DATE: _____

Medial Consonants

Directions: Say the name of each picture. Draw a line from each picture to the letter of its middle consonant sound.

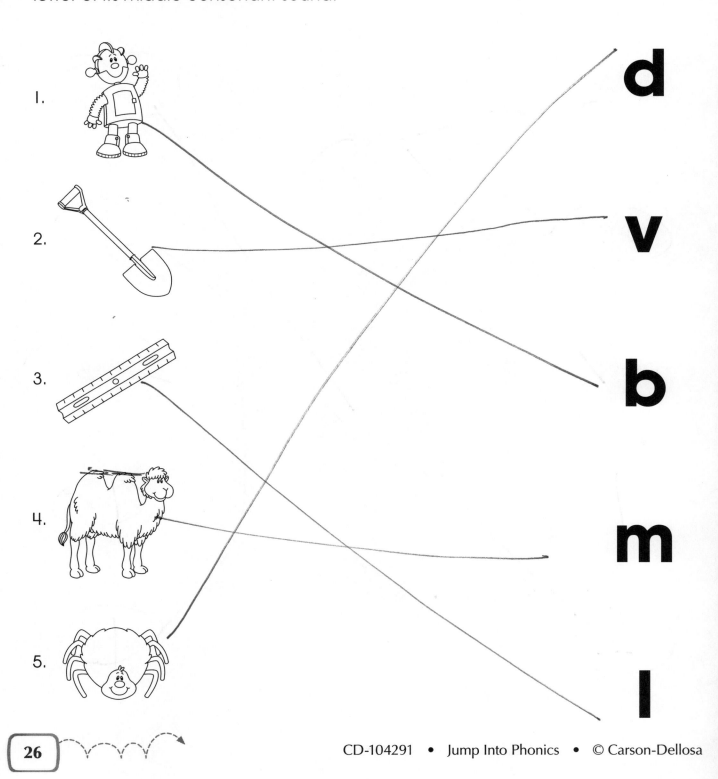

1.

2.

3.

4.

5.

d

v

b

m

l

CD-104291 • Jump Into Phonics • © Carson-Dellosa

NAME: _____ **DATE:** _____

Hard and Soft C

Directions: Look at each picture and say the word. Circle **hard c** if the word begins with the /k/ sound, as in *coat*. Circle **soft c** if the word begins with the /s/ sound, as in *city*.

1.

(hard c)
soft c   K
         S

2.

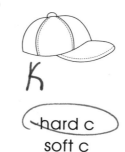

K
(hard c)
soft c

3.

S
hard c
(soft c)

4.

S
hard c
(soft c)

5.

R
(hard c)
soft c

6.

R
(hard c)
soft c

7.

C S
hard c
(soft c)

8.

R
(hard c)
soft c

9.

K
(hard c)
soft c

Consonants

Hard and Soft G

Directions: Say each word in the word box. If the *g* makes the /g/ sound, as in *gum*, write the word under the picture of the gum. If the *g* makes the /j/ sound, as in *giraffe*, write the word under the picture of the giraffe.

WORD BOX

game	gate	gem	germ
giant	gold	guitar	gym

game

gate

gold

guitar

Bem

germ

giant

gym

NAME: _____   DATE: _____

Hard and Soft G

Directions: Say the name of each picture. Circle **hard g** if the word begins with the /g/ sound, as in *gate*. Circle **soft g** if the word begins with the /j/ sound, as in *germ*.

1.
~~hard g~~
soft g

2.
hard g
~~soft g~~

3.
~~hard g~~
soft g

4.
hard g
~~soft g~~

5.
~~hard g~~
soft g

6.
~~hard g~~
soft g

7.
~~hard g~~
soft g

8.
~~hard g~~
soft g

9.
~~hard g~~
soft g

Consonants Review

Directions: Say the name of each picture. Circle the letter of the beginning sound.

1.

    z   v

2.

    l   m

3.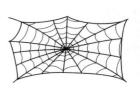

    c   w

Directions: Say the name of each picture. Circle the letter of the ending sound.

4.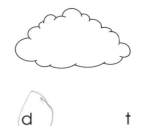

    d   t

5.

    n   p

6.

    l   y

Directions: Say the name of each picture. Fill in the blanks with the letters of the middle consonant sound.

7.  ra __b__ __b__ it

8.  mi __r__ __r__ or

9.  wa __f__ __f__ les

10.  la __d__ __d__ er

CD-104291 • Jump Into Phonics • © Carson-Dellosa

Consonants Review

Directions: Say the name of each picture. Circle the words with the same beginning sound.

1.

   (bat)
   book
   vase

2.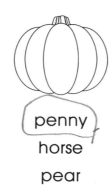

   (penny)
   horse
   pear

3.

   lemon
   duck
   ladder

Directions: Say the name of each picture. Circle the words with the same ending sound.

4.

   (balloon)
   mitten
   (fork)

5.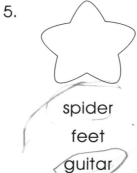

   spider
   feet
   (guitar)

6.

   dog
   (hat)
   (boat)

Directions: Say the name of each picture. Circle the words with the same middle consonant sound.

7.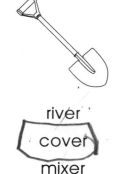

   river
   (cover)
   mixer

8.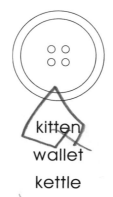

   (kitten)
   wallet
   kettle

9.

   (cabin)
   tiger
   robin

NAME: _____ DATE: _____

Consonants Review

Directions: Say each word in the word box. Write each word under the picture with the same beginning sound.

WORD BOX			
car	cat	cell	city
gate	gem	giant	gold

cake

goate

celery

cell

goat

gold

giraffe

gem

CD-104291 • Jump Into Phonics • © Carson-Dellosa

Diagnostic Test: Consonant Blends and Digraphs

Directions: Say the name of each picture. Write the letters that complete each word.

1.

   _Tr_ ee

2.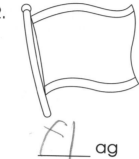

   _Fl_ ag

3.

   _Cl_ oud

4.

   _Sm_ ile

5.

   _Br_ oom

6.

   _Sk_ unk

Directions: Say the name of each picture. Circle the word with the same beginning sound.

7.

   (whistle)

   worm

8.

   candy

   (cheese)

9.

   (shark)

   sock

Directions: Circle the word that names each picture.

10.
bench

(leash)

11.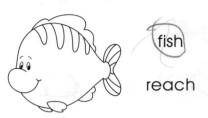
(fish)

reach

Directions: Circle the two pictures with the same ending sound.

12.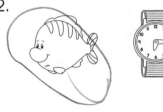

13.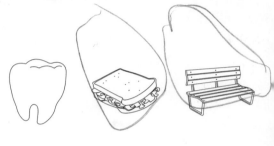

Directions: Say the name of each picture. Then, read the word. Circle the letter that is silent.

14. 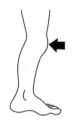 (k) n e e

15.  (w) r i s t

16.  (k) i c k

17.  c o m (b)

Directions: Check the boxes that correspond to correct test items.

Skill	Item Number					
Beginning Consonant Blends	1	2	3	4	5	6
Beginning Consonant Digraphs	7	8	9			
Ending Consonant Digraphs	10	11	12	13		
Silent Letters	14	15	16	17		

TOTAL CORRECT: _____

Teacher Notes and Activities

Consonant Blends and Digraphs

After students have mastered initial consonant sounds, you can begin to introduce initial consonant blends and digraphs. *Consonant blend* is the name given to two or three consonants that appear together in a word. Each consonant retains its own sound when blended. Initial consonant blends consist of three major groups: *l* blends, as in *cloud*; *r* blends, as in *train*; and *s* blends, as in *skirt*.

A consonant digraph consists of two consonants that make one sound when joined. The sound is often a new sound that is different from the sounds made by the consonants in isolation. The most common consonant digraphs are *sh*, *ch*, *th*, and *wh*.

Some consonant digraphs have silent letters. For example, the consonant digraph *kn* makes the /n/ sound, as in *kneel*, and the *ck* digraph makes the /k/ sound, as in *duck*.

Reinforce the difference between a blend and a digraph by displaying examples in the classroom. Fill a pocket chart with pictures and words that contain blends or digraphs. Use index cards to create letter cards for blends and digraphs. Cut the index cards between the letters of the blends to emphasize that blends retain separate sounds. Each digraph should remain on one index card to visually reinforce that it creates one new sound.

Students with limited English proficiency may struggle to grasp the concept of digraphs. Introduce examples of words that contain the same sounds. Place items such as cherries, a chair, and chocolate chips at a table. Write a label for each word and underline the digraph sound. To help students better understand each word in context, have them examine each item and say the sound aloud. Repeat this process for each digraph sound.

Unit II: Consonant Blends and Digraphs

Teacher Activity 1: Consonant Blend Adventure

Tell students to prepare for an adventure. Give students an atlas or world map and paper. Then, have them decide where they would like to travel. Students should choose destinations with consonant blends in their names. For example, students could plan trips to Florida, Spain, San Francisco, or Croatia. Once they have chosen their destinations, encourage students to create travel brochures for their locations. Have students underline and count all of the consonant blends that they find in their text. Record the results on a chart or bar graph on the board to find the total number of blends the class used.

Teacher Activity 2: Digraph Chains

Give each student several strips of red, yellow, blue, and green construction paper. Demonstrate how each strip can form a link, and the links can form a chain. Write the following digraphs beside a color name on the board: *ch*, *sh*, *th*, and *wh*. Each color should represent a different digraph. Explain that students should write a word with a digraph onto each paper strip. Once students have written their words, encourage them to form a pattern by combining their links. Link individual student chains into a class chain to display in the classroom.

Teacher Activity 3: R Blend Train

Draw a train engine and caboose on a sheet of construction paper and cut them out. Tape the train engine to a classroom wall and save the caboose for later. Challenge students to create the body of the train with words that contain *r* blends. Give each student a sheet of construction paper on which she can design and cut out a train car. Have students write a word that has an *r* blend on each car. Allow students to share the words they wrote before assembling the class train. Attach the caboose to the end of the train once all of the train cars have been displayed on the wall.

Teacher Activity 4: Word Wheel

Draw a large wheel with eight spokes on a sheet of paper. Write the letters *wh* in the center of the wheel. Make a copy for each student. Instruct students to write a different word that contains the *wh* digraph on each spoke of the wheel. Students can color their wheels before cutting them out and sharing them with the class.

Teacher Activity 5: Word Works

Punch a hole in the corner of a set of index cards. Give each student six to eight cards. Have students write a different blend or digraph on each index card. Explain that when you say a word, they should quickly identify the blend or digraph they hear and raise the matching card. Monitor students' answers, noting which students need additional review for specific initial consonant blends and digraphs. Students should attach the index cards together with metal rings or yarn to use for continued practice.

CD-104291 • Jump Into Phonics • © Carson-Dellosa

Unit II: Consonant Blends and Digraphs

Teacher Activity 6: Digraph Shopping List

Let students scan a variety of store catalogs and grocery circulars. Explain that they need to create shopping lists that include items containing digraphs in their names. For example, students could list items such as shoes, shirts, cherries, and chips. Allow students to share their shopping lists with the class.

Building Language

Note the following examples of words containing blends, digraphs, and silent letters. These sample words have been used throughout the book. Prior to teaching these letter/sound associations, familiarize students with the words to ensure that they hear each word sound and understand each word meaning.

L: blanket, blaze, blink, bloom, blue, clam, cloud, clown, flag, flame, flower, flute, fly, glove, glue plaid, plant, plot, plow, plum, sled, sleep, slide, slippers

R: branch, bread, brick, brush, crab, crayon, crib, crown, dream, dress, drill, drip, drum, frame, frog, grapes, grass, gray, green, grin, pretzel, prince, print, prize, proud, train, tree, truck, trunk

S: scale, scares, school, scout, shack, shore, skid, skim, skin, skip, skirt, sky, small, smart, smell, smile, smoke, smooth, snake, snap, snowman, spider, spool, spoon, swan, sweater, swing

SPL/SPR: splendid, splint, splinter, splurge, sprawl, spray, spread, sprinkle, sprint, sprout

SCR/STR: scrap, scream, screen, string, stripe, scrape, street, strong, scrub, straight

CH: bench, chain, chair, cheese, cherry, chimney, sandwich

SH: brush, fish, leash, shark, sheep, shell, shoe, shovel

TH: both, math, moth, thermometer, thimble, thorn, three, thumb, tooth, with

WH: whale, wheel, whisk, whistle

Silent letters: castle, comb, kick, knee, knit, knot, school, thumb, wrench, wrist

Consonant Blends and Digraphs

Consonant Blends: BR, TR

Directions: Write the word from the word box that names each picture.

WORD BOX

brush	train	trunk	truck
tree	branch	brick	bread

1. branch

2.  bread

3. 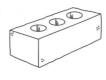 brick

4.  brush

5. 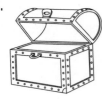 trunk

6.  train

7.  truck

8.  tree

CD-104291 • Jump Into Phonics • © Carson-Dellosa

Consonant Blend: DR

Consonant Blends and Digraphs

Directions: Write the word from the word box that completes each sentence.

WORD BOX			
draft	drape	dress	drip
draw	dream	drill	drum

1. Gwen is wearing a new _____dress_____ to the party.

2. Dad used a _____drill_____ to build Fido's new doghouse.

3. Doug wants a _____drum_____ set for his birthday.

4. Gayle had an amazing _____dream_____ last night.

5. We fixed the faucet when it started to _____drip_____ .

6. My uncle can _____draw_____ good pictures of people.

7. Mom closed the window when she felt a _____draft_____ .

8. Please _____drape_____ the sheet over the couch so that it stays clean.

Consonant Blends
and Digraphs

Consonant Blends: CR, FR

Directions: Say the name of each picture. Then, write the word from the word box that completes the sentence.

WORD BOX					
crayon	frog	crib	crab	frame	crown

1. Use the blue ___crayon___ to color the sky.

2. A baby sleeps in a ___crib___ .

3. Tonya bought a ___frame___ for the picture.

4. Abby saw a ___crab___ on the beach.

5. The king wore a ___crown___ on his head.

6. The ___frog___ sat on a lily pad.

CD-104291 • Jump Into Phonics • © Carson-Dellosa

Consonant Blends: GR, PR

Consonant Blends and Digraphs

Directions: Say each word in the word box. If the word begins with the /gr/ sound, as in *grapes*, write it under the picture of the grapes. If the word begins with the /pr/ sound, as in *pretzel*, write it under the picture of the pretzel.

WORD BOX			
grass	gray	green	grin
prince	print	prize	proud

grass

gray

green

grin

prince

print

prize

proud

NAME: _____ JM, _____   DATE: _2/6 2/23/22_

Consonant Blends: CL, GL

Directions: Say the name of each picture. Circle the word with the same beginning sound.

1.

crown

class

glow

2.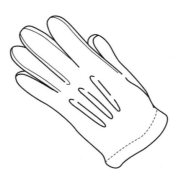

play

glad

plan

3.

place

green

gleam

4.

glad

slide

clap

5.

plenty

glance

grand

6.

globe

close

crayon

CD-104291 • Jump Into Phonics • © Carson-Dellosa

Consonant Blends: BL, PL

Directions: Draw a line from each word to the picture with the same beginning sound.

plaid   blanket

blue   plan

plot   blaze

bloom   plow

blink   plum

NAME: _____ DATE: _2/18_

Consonant Blends: FL, SL

Directions: Say the name of each picture. Fill in the circle next to the letters of the beginning sound.

1.

   ○ fl   ○ sl

2.

   ○ fl   ○ sl

3.

   ○ fl   ○ sl

4.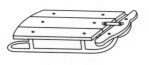

   ○ fl   ○ sl

5.

   ○ fl   ○ sl

6.

   ○ fl   ○ sl

7.

   ○ fl   ○ sl

8.

   ○ fl   ○ sl

9.

   ○ fl   ○ sl

CD-104291 • Jump Into Phonics • © Carson-Dellosa

Consonant Blends: SC, SK

Directions: Write the word from the word box that completes each sentence.

WORD BOX			
scale	school	skid	skirt
scares	scout	skip	sky

1. We put the apples on the _____ to weigh them.

2. The girls _____ home on sunny days.

3. There is not a cloud in the _____ today.

4. The thunder _____ my little brother.

5. She wore a sweater and a pretty _____ .

6. I am joining my school's _____ troop.

7. My _____ has a playground with three swingsets.

8. Be careful not to _____ on the icy road.

Consonant Blends and Digraphs

Consonant Blends: SM, SN

Directions: Say each word in the word box. If the word begins with the /sm/ sound, as in *smile*, write it under the picture of the smile. If the word begins with the /sn/ sound, as in *snail*, write it under the picture of the snail.

WORD BOX			
snack	small	smart	smell
smooth	snake	snap	snow

Consonant Blends: SP, SW

Directions: Write the word from the word box that names each picture.

WORD BOX		
spider	spool	spoon
swan	sweater	swing

1.

_____

2.

_____

3.

_____

4.

_____

5.

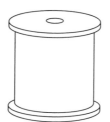

_____

6.

_____

Consonant Blends: SPL, SPR

Directions: Say each word in the word box. If the word begins with the /spl/ sound, as in *splash*, write it under the picture of the splash. If the word begins with the /spr/ sound, as in *spring*, write it under the picture of the spring.

WORD BOX					
splurge	sprint	split	splendid	splint	splatter
sprout	splinter	spray	spread	sprinkle	sprawl

Consonant Blends: SCR, STR

Directions: Read each word. Draw a line from each word to the picture with the same beginning sound.

scrap

screen   scream

straight   string

scrub   stripe

strong   scrape

street

NAME: _____ DATE: _____

Consonant Digraphs: SH

Directions: Say the name of each picture. Circle the pictures that make the /sh/ sound, as in *shoe*. Draw an X on each picture that does not make the /sh/ sound.

1.

2.

3.

4.
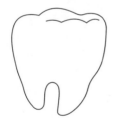

5.

6.

7.

8.

9.

CD-104291 • Jump Into Phonics • © Carson-Dellosa

NAME: _____ DATE: _____

Consonant Digraph: CH

Directions: Say the name of each picture. Circle the pictures that make the /ch/ sound, as in *chin*. Draw an X on each picture that does not make the /ch/ sound.

1.

2.

3.

4.
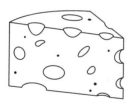

5.

6.

7.

8.

9.
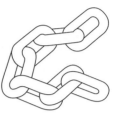

NAME: _____ DATE: _____

Consonant Digraphs: CH and SH

Directions: Say the name of each picture. Write **ch** or **sh** to complete the word.

1.

_____ imney

2.

_____ ovel

3.

bru _____

4.
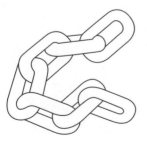
_____ oe

5.

_____ ark

6.

_____ erry

7.

_____ ain

8.

sandwi _____

9.

ben _____

Consonant Digraph: WH

Directions: Say the name of each picture. Circle the pictures that make the /hw/ sound, as in *wheat*. Draw an X on each picture that does not make the /hw/ sound.

1.

2.

3.

4.

5.

6.

7.
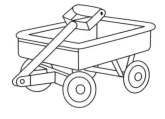

8.
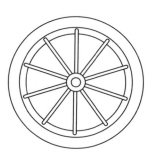

9.

Consonant Blends and Digraphs

Consonant Digraph: TH

Directions: Say each word. If the /th/ sound is at the beginning of the word, draw a line to the thimble. If the /th/ sound is at the end if the word, draw a line to the tooth.

thorn   math

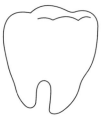

thirty   thumb

thermometer   moth

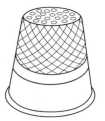

both   with

Silent Letters

Directions: Say the name of each picture. Then, read the word. Circle the letter that is silent.

Sometimes, words have letters that are silent. For example, look at and say the word *knit*. You do not hear the /k/ sound, but the *k* is part of the word.

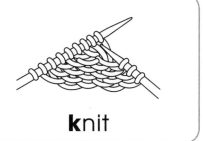

knit

1.

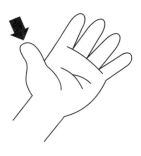

w r i s t

2.

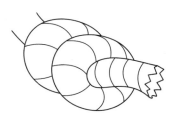

k n o t

3.

c o m b

4.

t h u m b

5.

w r e n c h

6.

c a s t l e

Silent Letters

Directions: Fill in the blank with the correctly spelled missing word.

Sometimes, words have letters that are silent. For example, look at and say the word *school*. You do not hear the /h/ sound, but the *h* is part of the word.

sc**h**ool

1. Sara will _____ a new toy for the contest.
   (desine, design, desing)

2. The music teacher played the _____ on the piano.
   (chord, cord, kord)

3. The princess lived in a _____ on a hill.
   (kasle, casel, castle)

4. Please note the location of each exit _____ .
   (sien, sign, sine)

5. I have a loud _____ that I use at soccer practice.
   (whistle, wissel, whisle)

6. If you shout in a cave, you can hear an _____ .
   (ecko, eko, echo)

 CD-104291 • Jump Into Phonics • © Carson-Dellosa

Consonant Blends: Review

Directions: Say the name of each picture. Circle the letters of each beginning sound.

1.

cl   sl

2.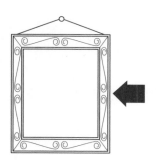

fr   fl

3.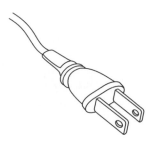

pl   sl

4.

gl   pl

5.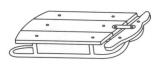

sl   fl

6.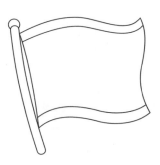

fl   fr

7.

cr   gr

8.

st   sp

9.

dr   br

Consonant Blends: Review

Directions: Say the name of each picture. Write the letters that complete the word.

1.

_____ own

2.

_____ apes

3.

_____ y

4.

_____ ead

5.

_____ ove

6.

_____ og

7.

_____oud

8.

_____ ock

9.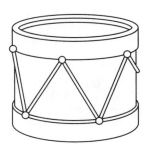

_____ um

CD-104291 • Jump Into Phonics • © Carson-Dellosa

Silent Letters: Review

Directions: Say the name of each picture. Circle the letter that is silent.

1.

s   t

2.

w   r

3.

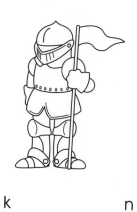

k   n

4.

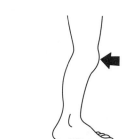

k   n

5.

m   b

6.

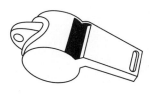

s   t

7.

w   r

8.

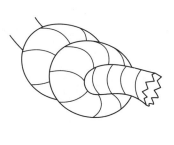

k   n

9.

w   r

Consonant Digraphs: Review

Directions: Write the word from the word box that names each picture.

WORD BOX		
wheel	thermometer	cheese
whistle	thimble	cherry
shark	chair	shell

1.

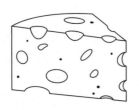

_____

2.

_____

3.

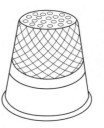

_____

4.

_____

5.

_____

6.

_____

7.

_____

8.

_____

9.

_____

CD-104291 • Jump Into Phonics • © Carson-Dellosa

Diagnostic Test: Short Vowels

Directions: Say the name of each picture. Draw a line from each picture to the short vowel sound in the word.

1.

ă

2.

3.

ĕ

4.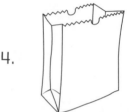

5.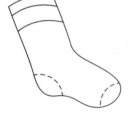

ĭ

6.

7.

ŏ

8.

9.

ŭ

10.

Diagnostic Test: Short Vowels

Unit III: Short Vowels

Directions: Write the word from the word box that names each picture.

WORD BOX

log	wig	cat
pen	bus	fish

11.

_____

12.

_____

13.

_____

14.

_____

15.

_____

16.

_____

Teacher Assessment Area

Directions: Check the boxes that correspond to correct test items.

TOTAL CORRECT: _____

Skill	Item Number			
Short Vowel a	4	7	12	
Short Vowel e	6	9	14	
Short Vowel i	3	10	15	16
Short Vowel o	2	5	11	
Short Vowel u	1	8	13	

Teacher Notes and Activities

Short Vowels

Learning short vowel sounds is essential to students' early reading and writing skills. Short vowel sounds are often introduced before long vowel sounds. When introducing short vowel sounds to students, explain that when there is only one vowel in a short word or syllable, the vowel usually makes a short sound. Short vowels often appear at the beginning of a word or between two consonants, as in the words *apple, fox, pat,* and *end*.

When teaching the short *a* vowel sound, tell students that it is the /a/ sound, as in *apple* and *mat*. When teaching the short *e* vowel sound, tell students that it is the /e/ sound, as in *egg* and *bed*. When teaching the short *i* vowel sound, tell students that it is the /i/ sound, as in *igloo* and *rip*. Many students confuse the /e/ and /i/ sounds, so additional review may be necessary. When teaching the short *o* vowel sound, tell students that it is the /o/ sound, as in *ox* and *pop*. When teaching the short *u* vowel sound, tell students that it is the /u/ sound, as in *umbrella* and *cup*.

Some short vowel sounds can change the sound of other consonants in the same word. Vowels *a, o,* and *u* make the consonant letters *c* and *g* hard. The *c* will make the /k/ sound and the *g* will make the /g/ sound, as in *can* and *gold*. Vowels *e* and *i* can make the consonant letters *c* and *g* soft. The *c* will make the /s/ sound and the *g* will make the /j/ sound, as in *cent* and *giant*.

To best reinforce short vowel sounds, display learning posters or charts around the classroom. Students can help create posters that reflect the short vowel sounds. Cut out shapes from card stock that exemplify the short vowel sounds. For example, an apple could be used for short *a*, an elephant for short *e*, an igloo for short *i*, an octopus for short *o*, and an umbrella for short *u*. Attach each shape to the top of a piece of poster board. Have students brainstorm words to create a list for each poster. The posters will provide a quick visual reference for short vowel sounds.

Pocket charts can also be used to reinforce short vowel sounds. Insert an index card into each row of a pocket chart to show each short vowel sound. Use the list of suggested short vowel words (page 67) to create a set of word cards. Have students insert the word cards into the correct rows. Then, leave the pocket chart on display as a reference.

R-Controlled Vowels

R-controlled vowel sounds should be introduced after students have mastered short vowel sounds. The letter *r* affects the vowel sound that precedes it. For example, when the letter *a* is followed by the letter *r*, the sound is changed to /är/, as in *star*. When the letters *e, i,* and *u* are followed by the letter *r*, the sound is changed to /ûr/, as in *fern, bird,* and *nurse*. When the letter *r* follows the letter *o*, the sound changes to /ôr/, as in *horse*.

Unit III: Short Vowels

Teacher Activity 1: Short Vowel Egg Hunt

Give each student several empty, plastic eggs and a small strip of paper for each egg. Have students write a word that contains a short vowel sound on each strip of paper. Students should write at least one word for each short vowel sound. Have students fill each egg with one of their short vowel words. Then, collect the eggs. While students are out of the classroom, hide the eggs. When students return, give each student a paper bag and let her hunt for the eggs. After all of the eggs have been found, have students open their eggs and read the short vowel words inside. For an additional challenge, have students sort the words by their vowel sounds.

Teacher Activity 2: Say and Sort

Divide the class into pairs. Give each pair a whiteboard, a write-on/wipe-away marker, and a dry eraser. Have one student in each group draw four lines on the whiteboard and write a vowel at the top of each column. Explain that one partner should say a word with a short vowel sound, while the other partner writes that word in the correct column. The activity continues as students take turns saying words and writing them in the correct columns. Create similar columns on the board and have each pair contribute a word to create a class list of short vowel words.

Teacher Activity 3: Silly Sentences

This activity shows how substituting one letter in a word can change that word's meaning and even the meaning of the sentence. Provide each student with a sheet of paper. Have each student write a sentence that contains a short vowel word, such as *"The nice lady has a silly cat."* Once each student has written his sentence, have him swap papers with a classmate. Students should circle the words with the short vowel sounds, and substitute other short vowels to create new words. In the example above, *cat* could become *cot* or *cut*. Students should rewrite the sentences, replacing the original short vowel words with the new words. Have students exchange papers again and share their silly sentences with the class.

Teacher Activity 4: Caps Everywhere!

Read the story *Caps for Sale* by Esphyr Slobodkina (HarperTrophy, 1987). Explain that you will create a tower of short vowel caps. Give each student five pieces of construction paper in the shape of a cap. Have students write a word containing a different short vowel on each cap. Have students sort the caps by their short vowel sounds. Then, create a giant stack of caps on a bulletin board or wall for each vowel sound.

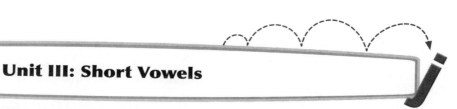

Teacher Activity 5: Sentence Stacks

Divide the class into groups of three or four students. Provide each group with 10 interlocking cubes per student and a variety of reading materials (e.g., textbooks, leveled readers, student magazines, and newspapers). Give students several minutes to search for short vowel words. To begin the game, one student should read a sentence containing a short *a* word, then remove an interlocking cube from the pile. The next student should then read a sentence containing a short *e* word, the next student a short *i* word, and so on. Each student receives a cube each time she successfully reads a sentence that contains the next short vowel sound. A student finishes when she collects 10 interlocking cubes. Play continues until all students have collected 10 cubes.

Teacher Activity 6: Short Vowel Sound Tubs

Fill a large plastic tub or bin with a variety of objects whose names contain short vowel sounds. For example, the tub could contain an apple, a hat, a bell, a shell, a bib, a lid, a doll, a lock, a brush, and a cup. Place the tub at a reading center and allow students to manipulate and sort the objects by their vowel sounds into five smaller plastic tubs. When all of the objects are sorted correctly, have small groups of students present the sound tubs to the class, announcing the short vowel sounds and naming each object in the tubs.

Building Language

Note the following examples of words containing short vowel sounds. These sample words have been used throughout the book. Prior to teaching these letter/sound associations, familiarize students with the words to ensure that they hear each word sound and understand each word meaning.

A: bag, bat, cat, hand, hat, pan, tack, van

E: bed, bell, belt, desk, dress, jet, leg, nest, net, pen, shell, step, ten, tent, test, web

I: bib, brick, dig, dish, fin, fish, hip, pig, sit, wig, zip

O: block, box, clock, dog, doll, fox, frog, lock, log, mop, rock, sock, top

U: bus, cub, cup, drum, duck, fun, gum, mug, rug, sun, truck

R-controlled vowels: car, bird, corn, door, farm, fern, fork, girl, horn, horse, jar, nurse, shark, star, thirty, thorn, turtle, yarn

Short Vowels

Short Vowel: A

Directions: Say the name of each picture. Circle the pictures that have the /a/ sound, as in *map*. Draw an X on each picture that does not have the /a/ sound.

1.

2.

3.

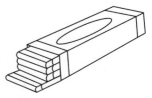

4.

5.

6.

7.

8.

9.

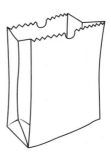

CD-104291 • Jump Into Phonics • © Carson-Dellosa

Short Vowel: E

Directions: Say the name of each picture. Circle the word with the **/e/** sound that names the picture.

1.

bed   bud

2.

jet   jut

3.

pen   pan

4.

bull   bell

5.

ten   tan

6.

nut   net

7.

nest   note

8.

log   leg

9.

wall   well

Short Vowels

Short Vowels: A, E

Directions: Say the name of each picture. Draw a line to the hat from each picture that has the **/a/** sound. Draw a line to the leg from each picture that has the **/e/** sound.

   CD-104291 • Jump Into Phonics • © Carson-Dellosa

Short Vowel: I

Directions: Write the word from the word box that completes each sentence.

WORD BOX			
bib	dig	fish	pig
fin	zip	sit	wig

1. Alissa wore a blond _____ with her costume.

2. Franklin wanted to _____ in the front row.

3. The baby wears a _____ when he eats.

4. I saw a dolphin's _____ out of the water.

5. My dog likes to _____ holes in the yard.

6. Jackie will see a _____ when she visits the farm.

7. It is difficult to _____ my coat when I am wearing gloves.

8. There are three _____ in the pond.

Short Vowels

Short Vowel: O

Directions: Write the word from the word box that names each picture.

WORD BOX					
block	box	clock	doll	fox	frog
lock	log	mop	rock	sock	top

1.

_____

2.

_____

3.

_____

4.

_____

5.

_____

6.

_____

7.

_____

8.

_____

9.

_____

10.

_____

11.

_____

12.

_____

CD-104291 • Jump Into Phonics • © Carson-Dellosa

Short Vowel: U

Directions: Say the name of each picture. Circle the pictures that have the **/u/** sound, as in *plug*. Draw an X on each picture that does not have the **/u/** sound.

1.

2.

3.

4.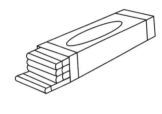

5.

6.

7.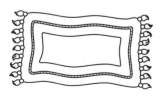

8.

9.

NAME: _____ DATE: _____

Short Vowels

Short Vowels: O and U

Directions: Say the name of each picture. Write **o** or **u** on the line to complete each word.

1.

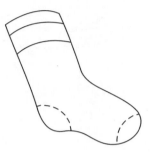

s _____ ck

2.

d _____ ck

3.

c _____ b

4.

l _____ g

5.

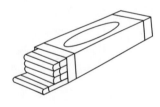

g _____ m

6.

cl _____ ck

7.

c _____ p

8.

fr _____ g

9.

tr _____ ck

CD-104291 • Jump Into Phonics • © Carson-Dellosa

Short Vowels

Short Vowels

Directions: Say each word in the word box and listen for the short vowel sound. Then, find each word in the word search.

WORD BOX

pan	dish	chick	clam	sock
nest	truck	belt	brick	frog
desk	mug	hand	doll	drum

```
s  x  g  x  y  s  w  j  e  n  d  t  w  s  z
s  g  h  c  h  i  c  k  u  t  e  s  z  i  j
g  g  c  d  a  t  d  f  t  n  p  g  x  a  e
b  l  v  d  n  i  j  r  h  a  o  j  l  c  j
l  l  p  v  d  z  c  o  s  j  y  e  q  v  e
y  y  f  y  h  p  l  g  c  e  d  e  s  k  m
h  v  z  t  p  t  s  r  c  b  r  f  h  u  b
z  w  o  f  k  c  r  h  y  p  m  n  r  y  f
t  z  l  c  p  z  c  u  k  g  t  d  d  w  z
c  p  o  c  m  o  a  c  c  x  o  h  o  t  v
d  s  a  o  o  y  i  z  f  k  j  o  l  p  o
i  s  n  n  l  r  b  p  o  y  m  e  l  m  b
s  c  n  e  b  f  a  n  x  c  b  r  a  b  z
h  u  c  r  s  o  d  m  u  g  a  l  v  z  l
r  t  h  x  g  t  b  l  d  f  c  c  x  v  u
```

NAME: _____ DATE: _____

Short Vowels

Short Vowels

Directions: Say the name of each picture. Then, write the vowel that completes each word.

1.

l _____ g

2.

c _____ t

3.

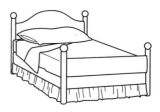

b _____ d

4.

c _____ p

5.

c _____ b

6.

p _____ g

7.

b _____ ll

8.

m _____ p

9.

r _____ ng

CD-104291 • Jump Into Phonics • © Carson-Dellosa

R-Controlled Vowels: ER, IR, UR

R-Controlled Vowels

Directions: Write the word from the word box that names each picture.

WORD BOX		
girl	fern	bird
turtle	nurse	thirty

1.

_____

2.

_____

3.

_____

4.

_____

5.

_____

6.

_____

R-Controlled Vowels

R-Controlled Vowel: OR

Directions: Write the word from the word box that names each picture.

WORD BOX		
horn	door	corn
thorn	fork	horse

1.

_____

2.

_____

3.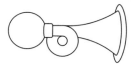

_____

4.

_____

5.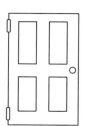

_____

6.

_____

CD-104291 • Jump Into Phonics • © Carson-Dellosa

Short Vowels and R-Controlled Vowels: Review

Directions: Say the name of each picture. Draw a line from each picture to its short vowel sound.

1.

ă

2.

3.

ĕ

4.

5.

ĭ

6.

7.

ŏ

8.

9.

ŭ

10.

Directions: Read each word. Circle the words with the /**ar**/, /**ur**/, and /**or**/ sounds.

11.
thorn	bone	rope	yarn
glass	perch	star	fern
turtle	story	girl	thirty

Short Vowels: Review

Directions: Say the name of each picture. Circle the letter of its short vowel sound.

1.

2.

3.

   ŏ   ă   ŭ   ĭ   ĕ   ĭ

Directions: Say the name of each picture. Write the letter of its short vowel sound.

4.

_____

5.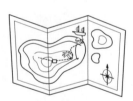

_____

6.

_____

7.

_____

8.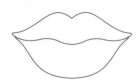

_____

9.

_____

R-Controlled Vowels: Review

Directions: Draw a line from each word to the picture with the same vowel sound.

surf

bear

barn

nurse

stir

fern

born

horn

chair

park

Diagnostic Test: Long Vowels

Unit IV: Long Vowels

Directions: Say the name of each picture. Fill in the circle next to its long vowel sound.

1.

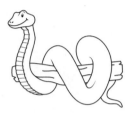

○ ē   ○ ā

2.

○ ū   ○ ī

3.

○ ī   ○ ē

4.

○ ā   ○ ō

5.

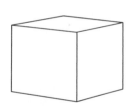

○ ū   ○ ā

6.

○ ī   ○ ū

7.

○ ō   ○ ē

8.

○ ō   ○ ū

9.

○ ē   ○ ā

CD-104291 • Jump Into Phonics • © Carson-Dellosa

Directions: Draw a line from each word to the picture with the same long vowel sound.

10. snake

11. bike

12. vine

13. grapes

14. hose

15. green

16. uniform

17. bugle

18. tree

19. soap

Teacher Assessment Area

Directions: Check the boxes that correspond to correct test items.

Skill	Item Number			
Long Vowel a	1	9	10	13
Long Vowel e	3	7	15	18
Long Vowel i	2	6	11	12
Long Vowel o	4	8	14	19
Long Vowel u	5	16	17	

TOTAL CORRECT: _____

Teacher Notes and Activities

Long Vowels

After students have mastered short vowel sounds, phonics instruction and activities should focus on long vowel sounds. Learning long vowel sounds is essential to students' early reading and writing skills.

Initial instruction for the long *a* vowel sound should focus on the following rules: When a word ends with a consonant and the letter *e*, the vowel *a* is usually long and the letter *e* is silent, as in *cake*. When two vowels are together in a word, the first vowel usually "says its name" while the second vowel is silent, as in *train*.

Initial instruction for the long *e* vowel sound should focus on the following rules: When a word only has an *e* vowel and it appears at the end of a word, the *e* is long, as in *be*. When two vowels are together, the first vowel usually "says its name" while the second vowel is silent, as in *leaf*.

Initial instruction for the long *i* vowel sound should focus on the following rules: When a word ends with a consonant and the letter *e*, the vowel is usually long and the letter *e* is silent, as in *bike*. When two vowels are together, the first vowel usually "says its name" while the second vowel is silent, as in p*ie*.

Initial instruction for the long *o* vowel sound should focus on the following rules: When a word has only an *o* vowel and it comes at the end of the word, the *o* is long, as in *no*. When a word ends with a consonant and the letter *e*, the vowel *o* is usually long and the letter *e* is silent, as in *nose*. When two vowels are together, the first vowel usually "says its name" while the second vowel is silent, as in *boat*.

Initial instruction for the long *u* vowel sound should focus on the following rules: When a word ends with a consonant and the letter *e*, the vowel *u* is usually long and the letter *e* is silent, as in *cube*. It is important to note that the long *u* vowel sound is traditionally pronounced /yo͞o/ However, there is an exception where the sound of /o͞o/ is referred to as a long *u* sound, as in *juice* and *tube*.

After students have learned long vowel sounds, activities can then focus on identifying the letter *y* as a vowel when it appears at the end of a word. There are two simple rules that reinforce this concept: The letter *y* makes the long *i* sound when it is at the end of a short word that has no other vowel, as in *cry*. When the letter *y* ends a word in an unaccented syllable, the letter has the long *e* sound, as in *funny*.

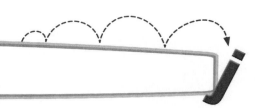

Unit IV: Long Vowels

Teacher Activity 1: Time for Long Vowels

Instruct students to write schedules of their daily activities that include long vowel words. Students should underline each long vowel word. Allow students to share their daily schedules with the class. Below is a sample schedule.

7:00 A.M.–<u>Wake</u> up; 7:30 A.M.–<u>Make</u> my bed; 8:00 A.M.–<u>Ride</u> the bus; 11:00 A.M.–<u>Writing</u> lesson; 3:00 P.M.–Soccer <u>game</u>; 8:00 P.M.–<u>Take a</u> bath

Teacher Activity 2: Long Vowel Baseball

Prior to this game, designate areas in the room to be home plate, the pitcher's mound, and the three bases. Divide the class into two teams and let them create team names. Explain that in this game of baseball you will "pitch" a word to a team member "at bat." If she can correctly name the long vowel sound in that word, then she has "hit" a single and can move to first base. If she can correctly name the long vowel sound and spell the word, she has hit a double and can move to second base. If a student misnames the vowel, she has "struck out." As each team scores a "run," record it on the board. Like traditional baseball, three outs signal a field change. Use the word list (page 88) along with additional long vowel words to challenge students' knowledge of the long vowel sounds. Play several innings and continue keeping score to determine the winning team.

Teacher Activity 3: Meet the Long Vowels

Students should enjoy creating books that introduce the long vowel sounds. Have students design a different page for each long vowel, and include pictures, words, and sentences that exemplify each long vowel sound. Allow students to share their books with friends in class or students in a younger grade.

Teacher Activity 4: Long Vowel Relay

Divide the class into five teams. Write the long vowels on the board. Have each team form a line and assign each team a different color write-on/wipe-away marker. Explain that one student from each team will race to the board and write a word containing a long vowel sound underneath one of the five vowel headings. Then, he will return to his team and give the marker to the next player. The next person in line should choose a different long vowel sound and write that word on the board. Students should be careful not to repeat words. The first team to write three words underneath each vowel sound wins. Remind students to be careful as they cross paths during this fast-paced relay.

Teacher Activity 5: Listen and Tally

Give each student a sheet of paper. Instruct each student to divide her paper into five columns by either folding it into five sections or drawing four vertical lines. Have students label the columns with the five long vowel sounds. Explain that you will play a few minutes of an audio book recording. Each time they hear a long vowel word, they should record a tally mark in the corresponding column. After a few minutes, stop the recording and have students count their tallies. Review their answers before replaying the audio recording and counting as a class.

Teacher Activity 6: Long Vowel Word Construction

Challenge students to brainstorm a class list of long vowel words and write their words on the board. Award students with one sticker for each word they contribute. Students can use their stickers to "build" the vowel of their choice on construction paper. Encourage students to take their letters home and tell family members what the stickers represent.

Building Language

Note the following examples of words containing long vowel sounds. These sample words have been used throughout the book. Prior to teaching these letter/sound associations, familiarize students with the words to ensure that they hear each word sound and understand each word meaning.

A: acorn, ape, apron, cage, cake, face, grade, grape, mane, paint, play, rake, snake, table, train

E: bean, bee, cheese, easy, green, key, knee, pea, queen, sheet, sleep, sneeze, tree, zebra

I: bike, dice, fire, five, hive, kite, light, lion, mice, prize, ripe, smile, spider, time, tire, vine

O: bone, cone, float, hope, hose, joke, note, road, rope, rose, soap

U: bugle, cube, humor, juice, unicycle, menu, museum, music, tube, ukulele, uniform, unit, vacuum

Y: baby, cry, city, dry, early, eye, family, fly, happy, my, sky, story, study

Long Vowel: A

Directions: Circle the word in each sentence with the /ā/ sound. Write the word on the line.

1. I hope that it does not rain today. _____

2. Holley and Lucas saw an ape at the zoo. _____

3. Jennifer rode on a train when she visited her cousins. _____

4. Wilson's pet snake is green and brown. _____

5. Mom asked me to set the table for dinner. _____

6. I can play tonight if I finish my homework. _____

7. The horse's mane is long and white. _____

8. I was happy with my grade on the test. _____

9. I finished all of the food on my dinner plate. _____

10. Jenny will bake a pie for dessert. _____

NAME: _____ DATE: _____

Long Vowels

Long Vowel: A

Directions: Read each word in the word box. If the word makes the /ā/ sound, as in *acorn*, write it beneath the picture of the acorn. If the word makes the /a/ sound, as in *fan*, write it beneath the picture of the fan.

WORD BOX				
cake	bag	cage	apron	rake
hat	paint	bat	candle	map

CD-104291 • Jump Into Phonics • © Carson-Dellosa

NAME: _____ DATE: _____

Long Vowel: E

Long Vowels

Directions: Say the name of each picture. Circle the pictures that have the /ē/ sound, as in *eagle*. Draw an X on each picture that does not have the /ē/ sound.

1.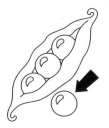

2.

3.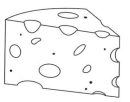

4.

5.

6.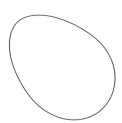

7.

8.

9.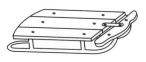

Long Vowels

Long Vowel: E

Directions: Say each word in the word box. If the word makes the /ē/ sound, as in *tree*, write it beneath the picture of the tree. If the word makes the /e/ sound, as in *leg*, write it beneath the picture of the leg.

WORD BOX				
queen	test	desk	sheet	nest
step	sleep	bean	tent	green

NAME: _____ DATE: _____

Long Vowel: I

Directions: Circle the word in each sentence with the /ī/ sound. Write it on the line.

1. Matt and McKenzie flew the kite in the park. _____

2. There are four pumpkins on the vine. _____

3. The car has a flat tire. _____

4. Davis rode his bike to the store. _____

5. The funny cartoon made me smile. _____

6. The bananas from the store were not ripe. _____

7. The winner of the poster contest will get a prize. _____

8. Dad will let us know when it is time for dinner. _____

9. Brianna has four mice and a turtle. _____

10. Turn off the light when you leave the room. _____

Long Vowels

Long Vowel: I

Directions: Say the name of each picture. Circle the pictures that have the /ī/ sound, as in *smile*. Draw an X on each picture that does not have the /ī/ sound.

1.

2.

3.

4.

5.

6.

7.

8.

9.

10.

11.

12.

CD-104291 • Jump Into Phonics • © Carson-Dellosa

NAME: _____ DATE: _____

Long Vowel: O

Directions: Say the name of each picture. Circle the pictures that have the /ō/ sound, as in *rope*. Draw an X on each picture that does not have the /ō/ sound.

1.
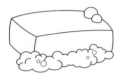

2.

3.

4.

5.

6.

7.

8.

9.
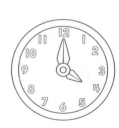

10.

11.

12.

Long Vowels

Long Vowel: O

Directions: Read each word in the word box. If the word makes the **/ō/** sound, as in *boat*, write it beneath the picture of the boat. If the word makes the **/o/** sound, as in *fox*, write it beneath the picture of the fox.

WORD BOX				
hope	clock	joke	road	doll
top	note	dog	box	float

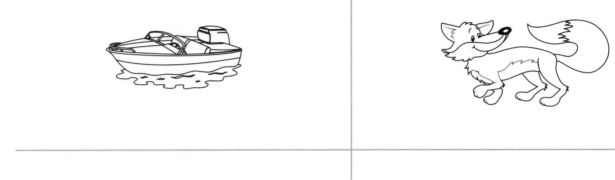

CD-104291   •   Jump Into Phonics   •   © Carson-Dellosa

Long Vowel: U

Directions: Circle the word in each sentence with the **/yo͞o/** sound. Write the word on the line.

1. The clown at the fair rode on a unicycle. _____

2. Lena's old uniform does not fit anymore. _____

3. My class did a unit on trees this week. _____

4. My class took a field trip to the science museum. _____

5. I enjoy listening to the music. _____

6. Keith has a good sense of humor. _____

7. Danielle's favorite instrument is a ukelele. _____

8. Everything on the menu sounded good. _____

9. Mom got a tube of toothpaste at the store. _____

10. I had toast and orange juice for breakfast today. _____

Long Vowels

Long Vowels: U

Directions: Say the name of each picture. Circle the pictures that have the /y<u>oo</u>/ sound, as in *bugle*. Draw an X on each picture that does not have the /y<u>oo</u>/ sound.

1.

2.

3.

4.

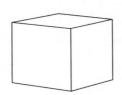

5.

6.

7.

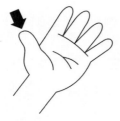

8.

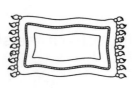

9.

NAME: _____   DATE: _____

Y as a Vowel

Directions: Write the word that completes each sentence.

Sometimes, the letter *y* is used as a vowel.
The letter *y* can make the /ē/ sound,
as in the word *baby*. It can also make the
/ī/ sound, as in the word *fly*.

 **baby**    **fly**

1. Mom and I were _____ for the baseball sign-ups.
   (early, earlee)

2. The _____ was dark, but it did not rain.
   (ski, sky)

3. The little brown _____ is my favorite one.
   (puppe, puppy)

4. The paint was not _____ yet.
   (dri, dry)

5. I _____ every night at the desk in my room.
   (study, stude)

6. Dana's _____ went to the mountains on vacation.
   (family, familee)

NAME: _____   DATE: _____

Y as a Vowel

Directions: Read each word in the word box. If the word makes the /ī/ sound, as in *fly*, write the word beneath the picture of the fly. If the word makes the /ē/ sound, as in *baby*, write the word beneath the picture of the baby.

WORD BOX				
sky	happy	city	early	eye
cry	story	my	dry	study

Long Vowels: Review

Directions: Draw a line from each word to the picture with the same long vowel sound.

zebra  spider

bike  cube

acorn  bone

music  face

robe  sneeze

Long Vowels: Review

Directions: Say the name of each picture. Circle the long vowel sound in each word.

1.

   ē   ū

2.

   ā   ē

3.

   ā   ō

4.

   ū   ē

5.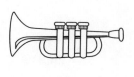

   ē   ī

6.

   ā   ē

7.

   ā   ē

8.

   ē   ō

9.

   ē   ī

CD-104291 • Jump Into Phonics • © Carson-Dellosa

Long Vowels: Review

Directions: Write each word in the word box under the picture with the same long vowel sound.

WORD BOX				
apron table	ripe broke	unit steep	key slide	grow uniform

_____   _____   _____

_____   _____

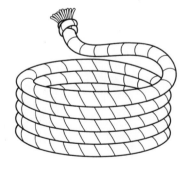   

_____   _____

_____   _____

Diagnostic Test: Vowel Digraphs & Diphthongs

Unit V: Vowel Digraphs & Diphthongs

Directions: Fill in the bubble next to the word that names each picture.

1.

○ boy
○ joy

2.

○ owl
○ towel

3.

○ house
○ how

4.

○ count
○ crown

5.

○ boil
○ bowl

6.

○ clown
○ cloud

Directions: Write the word from the word box that completes each sentence.

WORD BOX			
beach	grow	play	saw
float	knee	snail	pause

7. The _____ had a pink and brown shell.

8. Tom wants to _____ outside with his friends.

9. You can find many things in the sand at the _____ .

10. Sarah scraped her _____ on a rock.

11. Please _____ the movie while I get some popcorn.

12. Grandpa taught me to _____ on my back in the pool.

13. Mom will _____ tomatoes and lettuce in the garden.

14. Will and Deanna _____ a giraffe at the zoo.

Teacher Assessment Area

Directions: Check the boxes that correspond to correct test items.

TOTAL CORRECT: _____

Skill	Item Number			
Vowel Digraph ai	7			
Vowel Digraph ay	8			
Vowel Digraph ea	9			
Vowel Digraph ee	10			
Vowel Digraph oa	12			
Vowel Digraph ow	13			
Vowel Diphthong au, aw	11	14		
Vowel Diphthong oi, oy	1	5		
Vowel Diphthong ou, ow	2	3	4	6

Teacher Notes and Activities

Vowel Digraphs and Diphthongs

Once students are confident with short and long vowel sounds, it is important to introduce them to vowel digraphs and diphthongs. While the terms *digraph* and *diphthong* may be new to them, students will be familiar with these sounds.

A vowel digraph is a combination of two vowels where the first vowel is often long and the second vowel is silent. Many teachers like to coach their students with the following rhyme: *When two vowels go walking, the first one does the talking.* This rhyme teaches students that the initial vowel in the digraph is the one heard in the word.

The most commonly taught vowel digraphs include *ai, ay, ea, ee, oa,* and *ow.* When introducing the sounds, provide the following examples of vowel digraphs in use: *ai* as in *rain, ay* as is *hay, ea* as in *bean, ee* as in *feet, oa* as in *boat,* and *ow* as in *snow.*

When introducing diphthongs, explain that a diphthong is a combination of two letters, such as *oy* in *boy.* Tell students that when two vowel sounds come so close together, they are considered one syllable. A diphthong can be found in the medial position of a word, as in *coin* or *house,* or in the final position of a word, as in *cow* or *toy.*

The most commonly taught diphthongs include *au, aw, oi, ou, ow,* and *oy.* When introducing the sounds, provide the following examples of diphthongs: *au* as in *pause, aw* as in *jaw, oi* as in *join, ou* as in *out, ow* as in *cow,* and *oy* as in *boy.*

Both vowel digraphs and diphthongs will require extensive study and practice before students master these concepts. To provide a visual context for students, create a word wall that features these sounds. Create a header card for each digraph and diphthong. Attach the header cards to a bulletin board or empty wall space. Add words to the word wall as the class studies these vowel sounds. To help students with limited English proficiency, display pictures beside as many of the words as possible.

Unit V: Vowel Digraphs and Diphthongs

Teacher Activity 1: Vowel Digraph Highlighting

Provide each student with a sheet of white construction paper, two different colored highlighters, and an index card with a vowel digraph written on it. Have each student copy words containing her vowel digraph from the classroom word wall or from selected reading materials onto her sheet of construction paper. Then, have each student use one highlighter to mark the vowel digraph letters that match her index card. Use the other highlighter to mark the remaining letters. Let students share their highlighted vowel digraphs before displaying them in the classroom.

Teacher Activity 2: Diphthong Toss

Divide the class into groups of four or five students for this outdoor game. Provide each group with a few small beanbags and three or four circular objects, such as a paper plate, a large poster board circle, and a hula hoop. Each object should create a slightly larger circle than the one before it. Place an index card containing a diphthong, such as *oi, oy, ou,* and *ow,* in each circle. Have team members alternate throwing a beanbag into the circle of their choice. If his beanbag lands in a circle, the student should say a word that contains that diphthong. If a student says an incorrect word, he may have a second chance. Play until each student has had the opportunity to name several words. Record any new words on the classroom word wall.

Teacher Activity 3: Clay Digraphs

Students can practice their vowel digraph sounds with this kinesthetic activity. Provide each student with a small ball of modeling clay. Remind students that a vowel digraph is when two vowels are beside each other in a word or syllable. The first vowel is usually long and the second vowel is silent, as in the word *neat.* Explain that you will say a word that contains a vowel digraph. Have each student determine which two letters make the digraph sound. After students have determined the two letters, have them mold the clay to form each letter. Use the word list (page 108) as a reference as well as any additional words you feel will challenge students.

Teacher Activity 4: Coin Toss

Provide each student with a coin and a sheet of paper. Have students divide the paper into two columns. Tell students to label the left column with the diphthong *oi* and the right column with the diphthong *oy.* If the student flips the coin and it lands on heads, have her write a word that contains the diphthong *oi* in the left column. If the coin lands on tails, have her write a word that contains the diphthong *oy* in the right column. Encourage students to use library books and classroom materials for ideas. To conclude the activity, create a class list of the diphthong words on the board. Record any new words that can be added to the classroom word wall.

Unit V: Vowel Digraphs and Diphthongs

Teacher Activity 5: Take a Bow or Make a Bow

Students are often confused between the two sounds of *ow*. Create a picture card illustrating a person bowing and another picture card showing a gift with a large bow. Give students a stack of index cards printed with *ow* diphthongs or vowel digraphs. Have students place the index cards underneath the picture cards with the matching sounds. Once all of the cards have been used, have the class determine whether each word card has been correctly placed.

Teacher Activity 6: Creative Writing with Vowel Digraphs and Diphthongs

Challenge students to write stories that contain as many vowel digraphs and diphthongs as possible. Encourage them to copy words from objects in the room and from the classroom word wall. Once students have completed their stories, have them swap papers with classmates. Students should read their classmates' stories, then list all of the words they were able to find that contain either vowel digraphs or diphthongs. Encourage students to share how many vowel digraphs and diphthongs they counted.

Building Language

Note the following examples of words containing diphthongs and vowel digraphs. These sample words have been used throughout the book. Prior to teaching these letter/sound associations, familiarize students with the words to ensure that they hear each word sound and understand the meaning of each word.

Vowel digraph *ai*: braid, chain, nail, paint, rain, sail, snail, tail, train

Vowel digraph *ay*: clay, day, hay, pay, play, stay, tray, way

Vowel digraph *ee*: bee, cheese, deer, feet, knee, queen, seed, sheep, wheel, three, tree

Vowel digraph *ea*: beach, bead, beam, clean, dream, pea, sea, tea, team, seal, teach, treat

Vowel digraph *oa*: boat, coat, coach, float, foam, goal, toast

Vowel digraph *ow*: blow, bow, flow, grow, know, sow, show

Diphthong *au*: faucet, haul, launch, pause

Diphthong *aw*: claw, draw, fawn, paw, saw, yawn

Diphthong *oi*: boil, coin, oil, point, soil

Diphthong *oy*: boy, toys

Diphthong *ou*: cloud, house, mouse

Diphthong *ow*: clown, crown, cow

CD-104291 • Jump Into Phonics • © Carson-Dellosa

NAME: _____ DATE: _____

Vowel Digraph: AI

Directions: Write the word from the word box that names each picture.

WORD BOX		
snail	rain	sail
nail	train	braid
tail	paint	chain

1.

_____

2.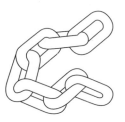

_____

3.

_____

4.

_____

5.

_____

6.

_____

7.

_____

8.

_____

9.

_____

© Carson-Dellosa • Jump Into Phonics • CD-104291

109

Vowel Digraphs and Diphthongs

Vowel Digraphs: EA

Directions: Draw a line to match the words with the /ē/ sound to the picture of the pea. Draw an X over words that do not have the /ē/ sound.

eat   clay

pen   each

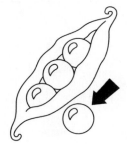

leaf   meat

tea   sail

bone   sea

CD-104291 • Jump Into Phonics • © Carson-Dellosa

Vowel Digraph: EE

Vowel Digraphs and Diphthongs

Directions: Write the word from the word box that names each picture.

WORD BOX		
bee	seed	deer
queen	wheel	feet
cheese	tree	three

1.

_____

2.

_____

3.

_____

4.

_____

5.
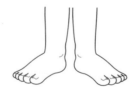

_____

6.

_____

7.
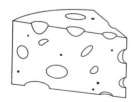

_____

8.

_____

9.

_____

Vowel Digraphs and Diphthongs

Vowel Digraph: EA

Directions: Write the word from the word box that completes each sentence.

WORD BOX			
beach	seal	treat	stream
team	dream	beam	cream

1. I like to make sandcastles at the _____ .

2. The tennis _____ won eight matches.

3. The _____ was my favorite animal at the zoo.

4. It was Cho's _____ to become a doctor.

5. The chocolate chip cookies were a special _____ .

6. My stepdad likes to put _____ in his coffee.

7. We set up our tent beside a _____ in the mountains.

8. The _____ of the car's headlights shone in the dark.

Vowel Digraph: OA

Directions: Draw a line to the goat from each word with the /ō/ sound. Draw an X over the words that do not have the /ō/ sound.

boat

float

frog

sock

coat

toast

knot

foam

coach

goal

Vowel Digraph: OW

Directions: Write the word from the word box that completes each sentence.

WORD BOX			
bow	grow	tow	slow
know	blow	flow	low

1. There was a bright green _____ on the gift.

2. I _____ that I will get a good grade on the test.

3. Wendy helped Adam _____ out his birthday candles.

4. Patrick liked watching his tomato plants _____ .

5. The river began to _____ again after it rained.

6. The opposite of fast is _____ .

7. The truck came to _____ our old car away.

8. The clouds are very _____ in the sky tonight.

Vowel Digraphs: AI, EE

Directions: Read each word in the word box. If the word makes the /$\bar{a}$/ sound, as in *snail*, write it beneath the picture of the snail. If the word makes the /$\bar{e}$/ sound, as in *tree*, write it beneath the picture of the tree.

WORD BOX				
tail	wheel	knee	rain	nail
sheep	deer	paint	bee	train

Vowel Digraphs and Diphthongs

Vowel Digraphs: AY

Directions: Draw a line to the hay from each word with the /ā/ sound. Draw an X over the words that do not have the /ā/ sound.

boat   clay

pay   coat

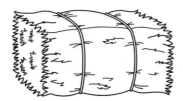

tray   coat

feet   play

way   beam

CD-104291   •   Jump Into Phonics   •   © Carson-Dellosa

Vowel Digraphs: EA, OW

Directions: Read each word in the word box. If the word makes the /ē/ sound, as in *pea*, write it beneath the picture of the pea. If the word makes the /ō/ sound, as in *bow*, write it beneath the picture of the bow.

WORD BOX				
bow	team	beam	sow	bead
know	clean	grow	blow	teach

Diphthongs: OI, OY

Directions: Say the name of each picture. Circle the pictures that have the /**oi**/ sound, as in *soil* and *joy*. Draw an X over each picture that does not have the /**oi**/ sound.

1.

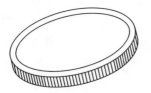

2.

3.

4.

5.

6.

7.

8.

9.

Diphthongs: OU, OW

Directions: Say the name of each picture. Circle the pictures that have the /ou/ sound, as in *how* and *count*. Draw an X over each picture that does not have the /ou/ sound.

6 G D

6 H D

6 I D

6 J D

6 K D

6 L D

6 M D

6 N D

6 O D

Vowel Digraphs and Diphthongs

Diphthongs: AU, AW

Directions: Draw a line to the saw from each word that has the **/au/** sound. Draw an X over the words that do not have the **/au/** sound.

haul

sail

launch

fawn

yawn

mark

clam

draw

claw

pause

Variant Vowels: OO

Directions: Read each word. If the word has the **/oo/** sound, as in *book*, draw a line from the word to the picture of the book. If the word has the **/oo/** sound, as in *moose*, draw a line from the word to the picture of the moose.

foot   igloo

boot   cookie

tooth   hook

look   spoon

roof   cook

Vowel Digraphs and Diphthongs: Review

Directions: Fill in the circle next to the word that names each picture.

1.

○ nail   ○ tail

2.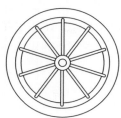

○ wilt   ○ wheel

3.

○ bow   ○ low

4.

○ boat   ○ bare

5.

○ teal   ○ seal

6.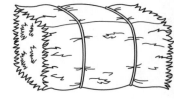

○ hay   ○ tray

Directions: Say the name of each picture. Circle the words in each row that have the same vowel sound.

7.   train   map   brain

8.   queen   bee   bell

9.   boat   toast   cot

Vowel Digraphs and Diphthongs: Review

Directions: Say the name of each picture. Circle the words in each row that have the same vowel sound.

1. boil   soy   lion

2. foil   day   joy

3.  gold   mouse   frown

4. house   clown   hawk

5. cow   claw   sauce

6. launch   yawn   sail

Vowel Digraphs and Diphthongs: Review

Directions: Write the word from the word box that completes each sentence.

WORD BOX		
rain	toast	team
hay	tree	show

1. I hope that it will not _____ on our picnic.

2. The horse likes to eat _____ and apples.

3. I watched a bird build a nest in a _____ .

4. My baseball _____ got new uniforms this year.

5. Darcy ate _____ and jam for breakfast.

6. I watch my favorite television _____ on Tuesday night.

Diagnostic Test: Word Study

Unit VI: Prefixes and Suffixes

Directions: Circle the prefix in each word.

1. review	2. misplace	3. unable
4. mistake	5. unclear	6. redo
7. unhappy	8. rewind	9. misspell

Directions: Circle the suffix in each word.

10. walked	11. fastest	12. singing
13. talks	14. bigger	15. foxes
16. dogs	17. greatest	18. jumped

NAME: _____   DATE:_____

Diagnostic Test: Word Study

Directions: Match the suffix or prefix to its meaning.

19. -ed

a. not

20. re-

b. past tense

21. -ing

c. more

22. mis-

d. bad

23. un-

e. again

24. -es

f. more than one

25. -er

g. action over time

Teacher Assessment Area

Directions: Check the boxes that correspond to correct test items.

TOTAL CORRECT: _____

Skill	Item Number			
Prefix re-	1	6	8	20
Prefix mis-	2	4	9	22
Prefix un-	3	5	7	23
Suffix -ed	10	18	19	
Suffix -est	11	17		
Suffix -ing	12	21		
Suffixes -s, -es	13	15	16	24
Suffix -er	14	25		

126   CD-104291 • Jump Into Phonics • © Carson-Dellosa

Teacher Notes and Activities

Prefixes and Suffixes

When introducing prefixes, explain to students that a prefix is a letter or group of letters placed at the beginning of a word to change its meaning. Explain to students that they can better understand word meanings by learning the definitions of different prefixes.

Show students how to determine if a letter or group of letters is a prefix or a necessary part of the word. Write the word *unwrap* on the board, then erase *un*. Students should confirm that *wrap* is a word by itself, meaning that *un* is a prefix that changes the meaning of the word. Next, write the word *uncle* on the board, then erase *un*. Students should note that the remaining letters do not form a word, therefore *un* is not a prefix in this instance. Remind students that just because a word begins with *re* or *un*, does not mean that these letters are functioning as a prefix. They should test each word to confirm that the beginning letters are indeed a prefix.

The prefixes *mis, re,* and *un* are among the most commonly taught. Other commonly taught prefixes include *dis, em, en, il, im, in, inter, mis, pre,* and *sub.*

When teaching suffixes, tell students that a suffix is a letter or group of letters placed at the end of a word to change its meaning. Explain to students that they can better understand word meanings by learning the definitions of different suffixes.

Students may sometimes be confused because a suffix often changes the spelling of the base word. Teach students the following rules: When a suffix is added to a word that ends with a *y,* such as *happy,* the *y* is changed to an *i* before the suffix is added. For example, *happy* becomes *happier.* When a suffix is added to a consonant-vowel-consonant (CVC) word, the final consonant is doubled before adding the suffix. For example, *sit* becomes *sitting.* When a base word ends with a silent *e,* the *e* is dropped before the suffix is added. For example, *bake* becomes *baking.*

The suffixes *ed, er, es est,* and *s* are among the most commonly taught. Other commonly taught suffixes include *ible, able,* and *tion.*

Display a poster with the most popular prefix and suffix meanings in the classroom. Below is a suggested list to include.

Prefixes: *dis* (not, opposite of); *en, em* (cause to); *in, im* (into); *im, in, ir, il* (not); *inter* (between); *mis* (wrongly); *non, un* (not); *re* (again); *over* (too much); *pre* (before); *sub* (under)

Suffixes: *ed* (in the past); *er, or* (person connected with); *ible, able* (can be done); *ing* (verb form); *ly* (characteristic of); *s, es* (more than one); *tion* (the act or process of)

Teacher Activity 1: Before or After?

Use the word list (page 129) for this activity. Tell students that you will say a word and they should either say the word *before* or *after*, depending on whether the word has a prefix or a suffix. Once students have learned to identify the location of the prefix and suffix, have them focus on using the correct term for each word. To help students make the connection between the words *prefix* and *suffix* and their locations within a word, have them transition from saying, "prefix-before" and "suffix-after" to "prefix" and "suffix."

Teacher Activity 2: Suffix Acrostic

Have each student write his name vertically on the left side of a sheet of paper. Challenge him to use a word or phrase that includes a suffix to describe himself. Below is an example to share with the class or use your own name as an example. Encourage students to share their poems before they are displayed.

T–thoughtful

Y–youthful

L–loving

E–extremely silly

R–respectful

Teacher Activity 3: Meaning Match

Create a set of index cards that contains either a prefix or a suffix and a second set that contains the corresponding definitions. Place the materials at a learning center. Challenge students to match the definitions to their correct prefixes or suffixes. Provide an answer key to make the activity self-checking. Review in class any prefixes or suffixes that are challenging for students.

Teacher Activity 4: Reduce, Reuse, Recycle

Explain to students that they can find examples of prefixes and suffixes every day in the world around them. Take students on a prefix and suffix scavenger hunt around the school. Have students bring clipboards to record any words with prefixes and suffixes that they find. (Check with the school office to be sure that students are allowed to browse the supply room, lunchroom, and other locations around the school during their search.) Once you return to class, have students share the words with prefixes and suffixes they found. Encourage students to extend this project outside of the school. Students can look for examples of prefixes and suffixes when riding in a car, reading at home, or shopping at the mall. Create a location in the classroom where students can share their findings.

Teacher Activity 5: Prefix/Suffix Switch

Tactile learners will benefit from this kinesthetic prefix and suffix activity. Give each student a sentence strip. Instruct her to cut the sentence strip into three equal pieces. She should then write a root word on each sentence strip piece. Provide each student with several small paper squares. Tell students to write either prefixes or suffixes on the squares. Students should place either the prefix cards or the suffix cards beside the sentence strip pieces to change the meanings of the root words. Note that not all prefixes and suffixes work with every root word.

Teacher Activity 6: What's in a Word?

This visual activity will help students better understand the concept of prefixes and suffixes. Create a table with seven columns on a sheet of paper. Moving from left to right, label the columns *word*, *prefix*, *root word*, *suffix*, *definition*, and *sentence*. Make a copy of the table for each student. Tell students to write words that include either prefixes or suffixes in the *word* column. Have students "break apart" each word by separating the root word from its prefix or suffix and recording the information in the appropriate columns. Then, have students write the definition of the original words and use them in sentences.

Building Language

Note the following examples of words containing prefixes and suffixes. These sample words have been used throughout the book. Prior to teaching these words, review the prefix and suffix meanings with students to ensure that they understand each word meaning.

mis-: misbehave, miscount, misjudge, mislead, misplace, misspell, misuse

re-: recall, recharge, reheat, reopen, replay, reread, restart, reuse, rewrite

un-: unable, unclear, undo, undone, unfair, unhappy, unlock, unlike, unsure, untie, unwrap

-ed: baked, biked, joked, laced, liked, promised, raced, raked

-ing: barking, batting, building, popping, reading, running, spinning, walking

-er: banker, farmer, player, speaker, singer

-er, -est: taller, oldest, bigger, funniest, neater, happiest, harder, tallest

-s (plurals): bees, bells, cats, dogs, frogs, hats, mugs, pigs

-es (plurals): boxes, branches, brushes, dresses, foxes, peaches

-s, -es: catches, hatches, helps, plays, stretches, works

Irregular plurals: children, dice, feet, men, mice, oxen, teeth

Prefix: RE–

Directions: Add the prefix **re–** to each word below. Write the new word on the line.

> The prefix *re–* means "to do again."
>
> re + make = remake (to make again)

1. read _____

2. play _____

3. write _____

4. heat _____

Directions: Complete each sentence with an answer from 1.–4.

5. Dad will _____ dinner once Mom gets home.

6. I asked Mr. Williams to _____ the story after lunch.

7. Jacob had to _____ his homework because it was messy.

8. Eli, Keira, and Morgan all wanted to _____ the game.

Prefix: UN–

Directions: Add the prefix **un–** to each word below. Then, write what the new word means.

> The prefix *un–* means "not."
>
> un + safe = unsafe (not safe)

1. sure _____

    _____

2. clear _____

    _____

3. well _____

    _____

4. able _____

    _____

5. known _____

    _____

6. like _____

    _____

7. happy _____

    _____

8. friendly _____

    _____

9. afraid _____

    _____

10. fair _____

    _____

Prefixes and Suffixes

Prefix: MIS–

Directions: Add the prefix **mis–** to each word. Write the new word on the line.

> The prefix *mis–* means "wrongly."
>
> mis + use = misuse (wrongly used)

1. lead _____

2. behave _____

3. place _____

4. spell _____

Directions: Complete each sentence with an answer from 1.–4.

5. Mom told us not to _____ when people visit.

6. I did not _____ a single word!

7. I do not want to _____ my umbrella on a rainy day.

8. The old map and directions _____ us.

CD-104291 • *Jump Into Phonics* • © Carson-Dellosa

Prefixes and Suffixes

Prefixes: RE–, UN–, MIS–

Directions: Add the prefix **mis–**, **un–**, or **re–** to each word. Then, write what the new word means.

1. done _____

2. use _____

_____

_____

3. call _____

4. like _____

_____

_____

5. judge _____

6. charge _____

_____

_____

7. make _____

8. count _____

_____

_____

9. play _____

10. cover _____

_____

_____

Suffix: –ED

Directions: Add **–ed** to each word in parentheses ( ). Write the new word on the line to complete each sentence.

> If a verb ends in a silent *e*, add the letter *d* to show that something has already happened.
>
> The boys tape the paper. The boys taped the paper.

1. Bob and Gus _____ to school this morning.
    (bike)

2. Then, they _____ home to watch their favorite show.
    (race)

3. The boys_____ up their shoes and went outside.
    (lace)

4. They _____ the leaves into big piles.
    (rake)

5. The boys _____ raking leaves.
    (like)

6. Then, they _____ some cookies with Gus's mom.
    (bake)

7. They talked and _____ the entire time.
    (joke)

8. Bob _____ that he would visit again soon.
    (promise)

Suffix: –ING

Directions: Add the suffix **–ing** to each word. Write the new word on the line.

The suffix -ing can be added to a verb to show action that is happening now. When a word ends in a consonant vowel consonant (CVC) pattern, double the final consonant before adding the suffix –ing.

consonant   vowel   consonant

tap + p + ing = tapping

1. run _____

2. pop _____

3. bat _____

4. spin _____

Directions: Complete each sentence with an answer from 1.–4.

5. I am _____ with my dog Patches.

6. The dancer is _____ and jumping.

7. My favorite baseball player is _____ right now.

8. The popcorn is _____ in the microwave.

Prefixes and Suffixes

Suffix: –ING

Directions: Add the suffix **–ing** to each word. Write the new word on the line.

When a word ends with two consonants or a consonant vowel vowel consonant (CVVC) pattern, add –*ing* to the end of the word.

consonant   consonant   consonant vowel vowel consonant

jump + ing = jumping   lead + ing = leading

1. bark _____   2. walk _____

3. read _____   4. build _____

Directions: Complete each sentence with an answer from 1.–4.

5. The puppy is _____ at a squirrel.

6. Dad and I are _____ a playhouse.

7. Holly and Alex are _____ the same book.

8. Spencer and Josh are _____ to the park.

Suffix: –ER

Directions: Add the suffix **–er** to each word. Write the new word on the line.

> Sometimes, the suffix –er means "one who does."
>
> teach + er = teacher (one who teaches)

1. speak _____

2. sing _____

3. farm _____

4. play _____

Directions: Complete each sentence with an answer from 1.–4.

5. The basketball _____ made a great shot.

6. The _____ has five cows.

7. My favorite _____ will be performing tonight on TV.

8. The _____ at my brother's graduation was funny.

Suffixes: –ER, –EST

Directions: Write the word that completes each sentence.

Sometimes, the suffix *–er* means "more." The ending *–er* can be used to compare two things. The ending *–est* means "most." The ending *–est* is used to compare more than two things.

When a word ends in *y*, look to see if there is a consonant before the *y*. If there is, change the *y* to *i* and add *–er* or *–est*.

The gray cat is furry. The tabby cat is furrier. The white cat is furriest.

1. Wilson is _____ than Owen.
   (tall, taller)

2. Alison is the _____ student in the class.
   (older, oldest)

3. The brown dog is _____ than the black dog.
   (big, bigger)

4. Doug's joke was the _____ joke of all.
   (funnier, funniest)

5. My sister's room is _____ than mine.
   (neater, neatest)

6. Diego was the _____ of all when he got his grade.
   (happier, happiest)

7. The math test was _____ than the spelling test.
   (hard, harder)

8. The tomato plant is the _____ plant in my garden.
   (taller, tallest)

Suffix: –S (plurals)

Directions: Add the suffix **–s** to each word. Write the new word on the line.

> Add the suffix –s to some nouns to show more than one.
> cat + s = cats

1.

dog

_____

2.
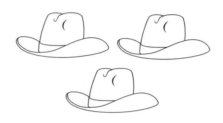

hat

_____

3.

bell

_____

4.

frog

_____

5.

pig

_____

6.

mug

_____

Suffix: –ES (plurals)

Directions: Add the suffix **–es** to each word. Write the new word on the line.

Add the suffix –es to words ending in *ch*, *sh*, *ss*, and *x* to show more than one.

beach + es = beaches   wish + es = wishes

class + es = classes   mix + es = mixes

1.

fox

_____

2.

dress

_____

3.

branch

_____

4.
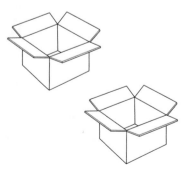

peach

_____

5.

box

_____

6.

brush

_____

Suffixes: –S, –ES

Directions: Add the suffix **–s** or **–es** to each word. Write the new word on the line to complete each sentence.

> Add the suffix *–s* to many verbs to show what is happening now. For verbs ending with *ch, s, sh,* and *x,* add the suffix *–es.*
>
> Bob (talk) to his mother. Bob talks to his mother.
>
> Marcy (wash) the car. Marcy washes the car.

1. The bird _____ from the brown egg.
   (hatch)

2. Bryson _____ on his homework every afternoon.
   (work)

3. The tiny gray kitten _____ with the toy mouse.
   (play)

4. The dog _____ the ball in its mouth.
   (catch)

5. David _____ his mother make dinner.
   (help)

6. Norah _____ before the big race.
   (stretch)

Suffixes: Irregular Plurals

Directions: Say the name of each picture. Circle the plural form of each word.

Sometimes, to show more than one, you have to make a new word.

mouse → mice

1.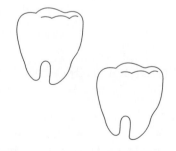

dices   dice

2.

oxes   oxen

3.

children   childs

4.

teeth   tooths

5.

feet   foots

6.

men   mans

Prefixes and Suffixes: Review

Directions: Circle the prefix in each word. Then, match the word to its meaning.

1. reopen   a. to write again

2. unhappy   b. not happy

3. misplace   c. wrongly used

4. unsure   d. to open again

5. misuse   e. not sure

6. rewrite   f. wrongly placed

Directions: Write the word that completes each sentence.

7. Walt runs _____ than Steven .
                        (faster, fastest)

8. My grandmother is the _____ person that I know.
                              (wiser, wisest)

9. Lee is the _____ student in his class.
                      (taller, tallest)

10. Dakota sings _____ than Alice.
                          (louder, loudest)

Prefixes and Suffixes: Review

Directions: Circle the correct word for each picture.

1.

mouse   mice

2.

banana   bananas

3.

book   books

4.

dress   dresses

5.

bee   bees

6.

ox   oxen

7.

pie   pies

8.
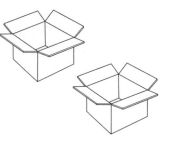

box   boxes

9.

spoon   spoons

CD-104291 • Jump Into Phonics • © Carson-Dellosa

Prefixes and Suffixes: Review

Directions: Write the word from the word box that completes each sentence.

WORD BOX		
banker	oldest	cats
restart	unsure	misplace

1. Dillon will start the movie again.

   Dillon will _____ the movie.

2. Mikaela has a gray cat, a tabby cat, and a white cat.

   Mikaela has three _____ .

3. Brendan is not sure what time the game starts.

   Brendan is _____ of what time the game starts.

4. Emma, Louis, Greg, and Marta are all younger than Doug.

   Doug is the _____ of them all.

5. José works in a bank.

   José is a _____ .

6. Try not to lose your scarf.

   Try not to _____ your scarf.

Diagnostic Test: Exploring Words and Word Parts

Unit VII: Exploring Words and Word Parts

Directions: Write a contraction for each pair of words. Write the new word on the line.

1. did not

_____

2. here is

_____

3. you will

_____

4. she would

_____

5. you are

_____

6. he would

_____

7. she is

_____

8. you would

_____

9. they are

_____

10. we are

_____

11. we will

_____

12. they would

_____

Directions: Use a slash (/) to divide each word into syllables.

13.

p e n c i l

14.

r a b b i t

15.

s k a t e b o a r d

16.

r o b o t

Directions: Circle the pair of homophones in each sentence. Circle *yes* if they are used correctly in the sentence. Circle *no* if they are not used correctly in the sentence.

17.   The night rode his horse into the knight.   yes   no

18.   Holly spilled flour on the flower.   yes   no

19.   The wind blue through the blew sky.   yes   no

20.   Travis felt weak for a week after he had the flu.   yes   no

Directions: Circle the correct homophone for each picture.

21.

bare   bear

22.

eye   I

23.

aunt   ant

24.

ate   eight

25.

flower   flour

26.

pear   pair

Directions: Say each word. Write the number of syllables that you hear.

27. tiger _____

28. acorn _____

29. favorite _____

30. desk _____

31. airplane _____

32. camera _____

33. mitten _____

34. shoe _____

Directions: Use a slash (/) to divide each word into syllables.

35. m o t o r

36. p a n c a k e

37. b i c y c l e

38. c a m e l

39. o c t o p u s

40. p i l l o w

41. p i c n i c

42. b a s e b a l l

43. d i n o s a u r

44. s t r a w b e r r y

Teacher Assessment Area

Directions: Check the boxes that correspond to correct test items.

TOTAL CORRECT: _____

Skill	Item Number				
Contractions: is	2	7			
Contractions: are	5	9	10		
Contractions: not	1				
Contractions: will	3	11			
Contractions: would	4	6	8	12	
Syllabication	13–16	27–44			
Homophones	17–26				

Teacher Notes and Activities

Exploring Words and Word Parts

Contractions

When introducing contractions to students, explain that a contraction is one word that has been formed by combining two words. Contractions are common in speech and in informal writing.

Explain that when writing a contraction, letters from the second word are removed and replaced with an apostrophe. Demonstrate this rule by explaining that the contraction *don't* consists of the words *do* and *not*. When combined, the letter *o* is removed from *not* and replaced with an apostrophe. The only exception to this rule is *won't*, a combination of *will* and *not*. This contraction is irregular and does not follow the traditional rules.

Syllabication

Explain to students that a word can be divided into units called syllables. All words contain at least one syllable. A syllable forms a word or a word segment. Explain to students that there are several rules regarding syllables. The first rule is the VC/CV rule—meaning to divide words between consonants to form syllables. An example of this rule would be the word *insect* (in/sect). The second rule is the V/CV division rule—meaning that when there is a consonant between two vowels, the word is divided after the first vowel if it is long. An example of this rule is the word *robot* (ro/bot). The third rule is the VC/V division rule—meaning that when there is a consonant between two vowels, the word is divided after the consonant if the first vowel is short. An example of this rule is the word *camel* (cam/el). Explain to students that the fourth rule is the most difficult because it is not reliable. The fourth rule is the V/V rule—meaning that the syllable division occurs between two vowels. An example of this rule would be the word *poem* (po/em). The fifth rule is the compound word rule. A compound word is divided between the two smaller words that make the compound word, if the two smaller words are each one syllable. An example of this rule is the word *doghouse* (dog/house).

Syllabication is a skill that relies heavily on auditory practice. Teaching the rules will aid visual learners, and integrating clapping and snapping will be necessary for tactile learners.

Homophones

When introducing homophones to students, explain that homophones are words that sound the same but have different spellings and different meanings. The words *sea* and *see* are examples of homophones. Homophones can be challenging for students because they are often misused and misspelled in writing.

When teaching these skills, it is important to integrate multiple techniques to reach all three learning styles. Creating a visual display for each skill will provide a quick point of reference for all students. Use a pocket chart to display letter cards that can be manipulated to form contractions. Integrate a listening center in your classroom to reinforce syllabication skills. Record yourself reading multiple syllable words. Instruct students to listen to the recording and clap or snap for each syllable they hear. Homophones can be reinforced kinesthetically by implementing photographs and word cards. Challenge students to pair the pictures with the correct word cards. Have students match each word card to the correct homophone.

Teacher Activity 1: Clap the Syllables

Use the word list (page 153) as a reference as well as any additional multiple syllable words you feel will challenge students. Tell students that you will provide a word clue or definition and they should clap the number of syllables in their answers. Select a student who clapped the correct number of syllables to share his guess. If he answered correctly, allow him to read the next clue. Continue the activity until students have had sufficient practice listening for and segmenting syllables.

Teacher Activity 2: Contraction Mittens

Give each student two mittens cut from construction paper and a circle cut from white construction paper for a "snowball." Tell each student to choose a contraction and write it on the snowball. She should write the two words that make the contraction on the mittens. Have students glue the mittens and snowballs on blue construction paper. Allow students to share their creations with the class before displaying them.

Teacher Activity 3: Homophone Memory Match

Have students brainstorm a list of homophones and write the list on the board. Divide students into pairs. Have each pair write the homophones on separate index cards. Shuffle both sets of index cards and place them in rows facedown on a table. Students should alternately draw a card and attempt to find its matching homophone. If the cards do not match, students should return them facedown to their original locations. Each time a student finds a match, he keeps the homophone cards. The student who finds the most matches wins. Allow students to play again for extra practice.

Teacher Activity 4: Contraction Puzzle

Cut sheets of poster board into enough rectangles for the contractions on the word list (page 153). Using a marker, write a contraction on each rectangle. Make various curved, zigzag, diagonal, and straight cuts between the letters to form a simple puzzle. Place the puzzle pieces in a bag. Then, place the puzzle bags at a learning center. Tell students that they should solve the puzzles and make lists of the contractions they found. Invite each student to write a contraction on the board.

Teacher Activity 5: Homophone Building

For this game, divide the class into groups of four or five students. Provide each group with a box of wooden craft sticks, washable markers, a small brown paper bag, and the homophone list (page 153). Have students work within their small groups to write each letter of the homophones on a separate craft stick. Before the game, have students practice spelling homophones with their letter sticks. Have students double-check their spelling against the homophone list to be sure all words are spelled correctly.

Explain to students that the object of the game is to build a homophone. Have students take turns drawing one letter stick from the bag. On subsequent turns, students may choose to return one unwanted stick in exchange for drawing two new letter sticks. To earn a complete match, a student must spell both matching homophones. Play is complete when all words have been formed and matched to their homophones. The student who creates the most matches wins.

Teacher Activity 6: Contraction Creation

Kinesthetic learners will benefit from this hands-on approach to understanding contractions. Give each student two sheets of copy paper, one sheet of construction paper, scissors, a glue stick, and uncooked elbow macaroni noodles. Post a list of paired words that form contractions on the board. Instruct students to choose a pair of words and write one word on each piece of copy paper. Demonstrate how letters are removed, usually from the second word, to form the contraction. Have students cut away the necessary letters to form the contraction. Explain that an apostrophe replaces the missing letter(s). Students should glue the new words on the construction paper, using elbow macaroni noodles as apostrophes. Allow students to share their work with classmates.

Teacher Activity 7: Contraction Tiles

Distribute letter tiles and paper to students. Be sure to program several tiles with apostrophes. Challenge students to create contractions using the tiles. Allow enough time for students to create as many contractions as possible. Have them record their contractions on the paper. Invite each student to write a contraction on the board.

Teacher Activity 8: Silly Homophone Sentences

Challenge students to create silly sentences containing multiple homophones. For example, *As I ate chili, the chilly wind blew the blue ball*. Encourage students to illustrate their sentences. Compile the homophone sentences into a book to share with the class.

Building Language

The following words are examples of contractions, homophones, and multi-syllabic words. These sample words have been used throughout the book. Use the lists of words for review and skill reinforcement.

Contractions

Are: they're, you're, we're

Have/has: I've, he's, she's, they've, you've, we've

Is: he's, here's, how's, she's, that's, there's, what's, when's, it's, who's

Not: aren't, can't, couldn't, didn't, doesn't, don't, hadn't, hasn't, haven't, isn't, wasn't, weren't

Will: he'll, I'll, she'll, they'll, we'll, you'll

Would: he'd, I'd, it'd, she'd, that'd, they'd, we'd, you'd

Homophones

ate/eight	bare/bear	be/bee	blew/blue
close/clothes	dear/deer	eye/I	flour/flower
for/four	hair/hare	hour/our	knight/night
knot/not	pair/pear	plain/plane	read/red
road/rode	sale/sail	son/sun	tail/tale
their/they're/there	to/too/two	week/weak	wood/would

Syllabication

Compound words (two syllables): bath/tub, ear/muffs, note/book, rain/bow, sand/box, sea/shell, skate/board, snow/man, wind/mill

Compound words (three syllables): but/ter/fly, la/dy/bug, sun/glass/es

VC/CV words: bal/loon, but/ter, car/rot, cen/ter, din/ner, doc/tor, lad/der, let/ter, mit/ten, nap/kin, pen/cil, pep/per, pic/nic, pil/low, rab/bit, tar/get, wal/rus, win/dow, yel/low, zip/per

V/CV words: ho/tel, mo/tor, pu/pil, pi/lot, i/tem, fla/vor, o/pen, re/port, fa/mous, re/port, ro/bot, spi/der, su/per, wa/ter, ze/bra

VC/V words: cam/el, shiv/er, shov/el

Three-syllable words: al/pha/bet, bi/cy/cle, com/put/er, di/no/saur, el/e/phant, kan/ga/roo, news/pa/per, pi/an/o, to/ma/to, um/brel/la

Contractions: Not

Directions: Write a contraction for each pair of words.

> A **contraction** is one word made from two shorter words.
> When the two words are put together, a letter or letters are
> taken out and an apostrophe (') is put in its place.
>
> had + not = hadn't

1. Anton and Clark _____ seen my new puppy yet.
   (have not)

2. Dawn _____ feeling well today.
   (is not)

3. I _____ laughed that hard in days.
   (had not)

4. Ilene _____ remember where she left her lunchbox.
   (can not)

5. Jawan and Leslie _____ seen the new movie yet.
   (have not)

6. Nadia _____ bring the snacks today.
   (did not)

7. Oliver _____ told anyone about the surprise party.
   (has not)

8. Emma and Sabena _____ like the color orange.
   (do not)

NAME: _____   DATE:_____

Exploring Words
and Word Parts

Contractions: Not

Directions: Write a contraction for each pair of words.

A **contraction** is one word made from two longer words. When the two words are put together, a letter or letters are taken out and an apostrophe (') is put in its place. When the word *not* is used in a contraction, the apostrophe is put in place of the letter *o*.

would + not = wouldn't

1. are not

2. can not

3. could not

_____

_____

_____

4. did not

5. does not

6. do not

_____

_____

_____

7. had not

8. has not

9. is not

_____

_____

_____

10. was not

11. have not

12. were not

_____

_____

_____

156

CD-104291 • Jump Into Phonics • © Carson-Dellosa

Contractions: Will

Directions: Write a contraction for each pair of words.

A **contraction** is one word made from two longer words. When the two words are put together, a letter or letters are taken out and an apostrophe (') is put in its place. When the word *will* is used in a contraction, the apostrophe is put in place of the letters *wi*.

they + will = they'll

1. _____ bring you some flowers from my garden.
   (I will)

2. I know that _____ like the book as much as I do.
   (you will)

3. _____ do well on the test because he studied.
   (He will)

4. _____ see monkeys, elephants, and tigers at the zoo.
   (They will)

5. I hope that _____ be able to come to my party.
   (she will)

6. Do you think that _____ win the baseball game?
   (we will)

Exploring Words and Word Parts

Contractions: Has, Have

Directions: Write a contraction for each pair of words.

A **contraction** is made when two words are put together to make a new word. When the two words are put together, a letter or letters are taken out and an apostrophe (') is put in its place. When you use the words *have* or *has* in a contraction, the letters *ha* are taken out and an apostrophe is put in their place.

we + have = we've

1. _____ a nice swimming pool in their neighborhood.
   (They have)

2. _____ always been great at drawing and painting.
   (She has)

3. _____ always been a good friend.
   (You have)

4. _____ worked hard to get better at tennis.
   (I have)

5. _____ studied for the test, so I am sure he will do well.
   (He has)

6. _____ been planning this trip for weeks!
   (We have)

Contractions: Is

Directions: Write a contraction for each pair of words.

A **contraction** is made when two words are put together to make a new word. When the two words are put together, a letter or letters are taken out and an apostrophe (') is put in its place. When you use the word *is* in a contraction, the *i* is taken out and an apostrophe is put in its place.

here is = here's

1. _____ a good friend of Matilda's.
   (She is)

2. Sharon said that _____ going to be sunny today.
   (it is)

3. _____ the sweater that Wynona left at our house.
   (Here is)

4. _____ going to come to dinner?
   (Who is)

5. _____ Benji's favorite kind of cake?
   (What is)

6. Janet and I think _____ a terrific idea!
   (that is)

NAME: _____ DATE: _____

Contractions: Are

Directions: Write a contraction for each pair of words. Each contraction will be used twice.

A **contraction** is made when two words are put together to make a new word. When the two words are put together, a letter or letters are taken out and an apostrophe (') is put in its place. When you use the word *are* in a contraction, the letter *a* is taken out and an apostrophe is put in its place.

we + are = we're

1. It will not be long until _____ +on our way again.
   (we are)

2. _____ going to help paint the kitchen.
   (They are)

3. _____ going on the field trip, aren't you?
   (You are)

4. _____ both in the school play this year.
   (They are)

5. Gina said that _____ having pizza for dinner tonight.
   (we are)

6. I think that _____ a little taller than me.
   (you are)

Contractions: Would

Directions: Write a contraction for each pair of words.

A **contraction** is made when two words are put together to make a new word. When the two words are put together, a letter or letters are taken out and an apostrophe (') is put in its place. When the word *would* is used in a contraction, the letters *woul* are taken out and an apostrophe is put in their place.

I + would = I'd

1. _____ have been early, but Mom could not find her keys.
   (We would)

2. Susan said that _____ bring snacks to the party.
   (she would)

3. My friends said that _____ help me rake leaves.
   (they would)

4. I hoped that _____ like the video game too.
   (you would)

5. Ted said that _____ sign up for the team if I did.
   (he would)

6. I knew that _____ be a great idea to make Mom dinner.
   (it would)

Exploring Words and Word Parts

Contractions: Would

Directions: Write a contraction for each pair of words.

1. I would _____

2. he would _____

3. they would _____

4. it would _____

5. she would _____

6. we would _____

7. you would _____

8. that would _____

Directions: Write the contraction that completes each sentence.

9. Sadie said that _____ help me with my math homework.
(I'd, she'd)

10. Drew lost his umbrella, but he said _____ turn up.
(that'd, it'd)

11. Megan and Leona said that _____ be here soon.
(they'd, she'd)

12. Enrique said that _____ like to be a teacher one day.
(it'd, he'd)

NAME: _____   **DATE:** _____

Contractions: Review

Directions: Write a contraction for each pair of words.

1. I will _____

2. you would _____

3. he had _____

4. is not _____

5. they have _____

6. we are _____

7. she is _____

8. has not _____

9. that would _____

10. it is _____

11. could not _____

12. we will _____

Directions: Write the contraction that completes each sentence.

13. Brent told me that _____ going to play basketball.
(he's, he'll)

14. Carmen _____ remember where she put her keys.
(wouldn't, couldn't)

15. Dad said that _____ a terrific help around the house.
(I'll, I'm)

Contractions: Review

Directions: Draw a line to match each word pair to its contraction.

1. you are

2. we will

3. I would

4. has not

5. that is

6. they are

7. she would

8. he has

9. is not

10. we have

a. I'd

b. they're

c. hasn't

d. she'd

e. you're

f. isn't

g. we've

h. we'll

i. he's

j. that's

   CD-104291 • *Jump Into Phonics* • © Carson-Dellosa

Contractions: Review

Directions: Write the contraction that completes each sentence.

1. _____ time for my favorite TV show.
   (It's, It'll)

2. _____ help Ms. Janovitz decorate the classroom.
   (We'll, We've)

3. I _____ want any juice with my breakfast.
   (aren't, don't)

4. Edgar said that _____ share his snack with me.
   (he'd, she'd)

5. Penny _____ afraid to ride the roller coaster.
   (won't, isn't)

6. They look alike, but Gabe and Aaron _____ brothers.
   (aren't, won't)

7. Janelle said that _____make a green and blue scarf.
   (she'll, she's)

8. Neil said that _____ old family friends .
   (they're, they'll)

9. _____ forget to take your umbrella.
   (Doesn't, Don't)

10. _____ going to the museum on Friday.
    (We'll, We're)

Contractions: Review

Directions: Circle the second word that makes each contraction.

1. could + _____ = couldn't	not	are	would
2. he + _____ = he's	is	are	not
3. is + _____ = isn't	will	not	is
4. we + _____ = we're	are	will	have
5. she + _____ = she'll	will	was	would
6. you + _____ = you've	has	have	had
7. was + _____ = wasn't	not	had	would
8. who + _____ = who's	is	will	not
9. he + _____ = he'd	would	is	will
10. I + _____ = I'll	will	would	are

CD-104291 • Jump Into Phonics • © Carson-Dellosa

One-, Two-, and Three-Syllable Words

Directions: Say the name of each animal. Write the number of syllables that you hear in the box.

1.

   ☐

2.

   ☐

3.

   ☐

4.

   ☐

5.

   ☐

6.

   ☐

7.

   ☐

8.

   ☐

9.

   ☐

Dividing Two-Syllable Words

Directions: Read each word. Write its syllables on the lines.

> Words are often divided into syllables between consonants. For example, *apple* is a two-syllable word. It is divided into *ap* and *ple* between the two *p*s.

1. napkin
2. butter
3. window

_____ _____   _____ _____   _____ _____

4. mitten
5. yellow
6. picnic

_____ _____   _____ _____   _____ _____

7. doctor
8. letter
9. target

_____ _____   _____ _____   _____ _____

10. pillow
11. pepper
12. pencil

_____ _____   _____ _____   _____ _____

13. center
14. carrot
15. zipper

_____ _____   _____ _____   _____ _____

Dividing Two-Syllable Words

Directions: Rewrite each word. Use a slash (/) to divide the words into syllables.

Each syllable in a word contains a vowel sound. If the first vowel sound is long, divide the word after the vowel.

Example: ro/bot

If the first vowel sound is short, divide the word after the vowel and the consonant.

Example: cam/el

1. cabin _____

2. hotel _____

3. motor _____

4. tiger _____

5. pupil _____

6. shiver _____

7. water _____

8. flavor _____

9. open _____

10. shovel _____

11. pilot _____

12. report _____

13. item _____

14. money _____

Exploring Words
and Word Parts

Dividing Compound Words

Directions: Say the name of each picture. Circle the answer that shows the correct way to divide each word into syllables.

> Some words divide easily into syllables because they are made from smaller words. For example, *mailbox* is a compound word. It can be divided into *mail* and *box*.

1.

snowm/an

snow/man

2.

wind/mill

win/dmill

3.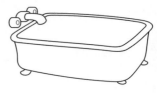

bat/htub

bath/tub

4.

noteb/ook

note/book

5.

sea/shell

seash/ell

6.

rai/nbow

rain/bow

CD-104291 • Jump Into Phonics • © Carson-Dellosa

Dividing Three-Syllable Words

Directions: Rewrite each word. Use a slash (/) to divide the words into syllables.

1.

bicycle

_____

2.

dinosaur

_____

3.

sunglasses

_____

4.
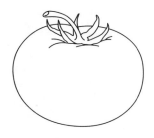
tomato

_____

5.

newspaper

_____

6.
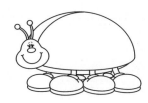
ladybug

_____

7.

elephant

_____

8.

piano

_____

9.

umbrella

_____

NAME: _____ DATE: _____

Syllabication Review

Directions: Read each word. Write its syllables on the lines.

1. dinner

___ ___

2. computer

___ ___ ___

3. pocket

___ ___

4. telephone

___ ___ ___

5. pencil

___ ___

6. famous

___ ___

7. sandbox

___ ___

8. cricket

___ ___

9. butterfly

___ ___ ___

10. camel

___ ___

11. alphabet

___ ___ ___

12. robot

___ ___

CD-104291 • Jump Into Phonics • © Carson-Dellosa

Syllabication Review

Directions: Rewrite each word. Use a slash (/) to divide the words into syllables.

1.

hammer

_____

2.

kangaroo

_____

3.

crayon

_____

4.

earmuffs

_____

5.

pumpkin

_____

6.

balloon

_____

7.

turtle

_____

8.

dinosaur

_____

9.

ladder

_____

Homophones

Directions: Look at each picture and read the words. Then, write a sentence using each homophone.

> **Homophones** are words that are pronounced the same, but have different meanings.

1.

ate   eight

_____

_____

2.

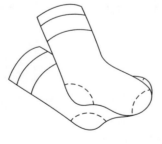   

pair   pear

_____

_____

Homophones

Directions: Draw a line to match each pair of homophones.

1. deer   a. sale

2. flower   b. son

3. plain   c. hare

4. road   d. weak

5. sail   e. blew

6. sun   f. flour

7. week   g. bare

8. tail   h. night

9. blue   i. dear

10. hair   j. plane

11. bear   k. rode

12. knight   l. tale

NAME: _____ DATE: _____

Exploring Words and Word Parts

Homophones

Directions: Write the homophone that completes each sentence.

1. Where will you _____ after school? (be, bee)
2. Watch out for the _____! (be, bee)
3. My aunt Nicole has _____ horses at her farm. (to, two)
4. Please pass these papers _____ Harrison. (to, two)
5. I _____ out the candles. (blew, blue)
6. My shirt is _____. (blew, blue)
7. My shoes are _____. (red, read)
8. I _____ that book. (red, read)

176
CD-104291 • Jump Into Phonics • © Carson-Dellosa

Homophones

Exploring Words and Word Parts

Directions: Write the homophone that completes each sentence.

1. _____ pack an apple in my lunch every day.
   (I, eye)

2. Some dust blew in my _____, and now it hurts.
   (I, eye)

3. Please _____ the window if it starts to rain.
   (clothes, close)

4. I have some new _____ to wear to school.
   (clothes, close)

5. There are _____ fish in the pond.
   (four, for)

6. I hope you like the gift that I bought _____ you.
   (four, for)

7. Put on some socks if your _____ feet are cold.
   (bear, bare)

8. The _____ cub at the zoo was cute and playful.
   (bear, bare)

Exploring Words and Word Parts: Review

Directions: Draw a line to match each contraction to its word pair.

1. don't   a. he is

2. I'll   b. we are

3. he's   c. is not

4. that's   d. I will

5. we're   e. I have

6. isn't   f. do not

7. they'll   g. you would

8. I've   h. that is

9. you'd   i. it is

10. it's   j. they will

 CD-104291 • Jump Into Phonics • © Carson-Dellosa

Exploring Words and Word Parts: Review

Directions: Write a contraction for each pair of words.

1. _____ going to the football game tonight.
   (I am)

2. Sue thinks that _____ be here soon.
   (they will)

3. Karen said that _____ read the book before.
   (she has)

4. _____ going to be a rainy day.
   (It is)

5. I am sure that _____ get good grades if we study.
   (we will)

6. _____ on my team at recess.
   (You are)

7. The movie _____ as good as the book.
   (was not)

8. Andre said that _____ bring juice to the party.
   (he will)

9. Chloe _____ remember the address.
   (does not)

Exploring Words and Word Parts: Review

Directions: Draw a line to match each pair of homophones.

1.	bear	a.	waist
2.	see	b.	hoarse
3.	waste	c.	rode
4.	fair	d.	sea
5.	horse	e.	write
6.	pear	f.	bare
7.	road	g.	night
8.	knight	h.	brake
9.	right	i.	pair
10.	break	j.	fare

CD-104291 • Jump Into Phonics • © Carson-Dellosa

Exploring Words and Word Parts: Review

Directions: Complete the story with homophones from the word box. Use each word only once. Not all of the words will be used.

WORD BOX					
blue	read	our	rode	sail	knot
blew	eye	hour	for	sale	would
red	I	road	four	not	wood

It was early summer. Boats drifted across the _____

lake. Rows of _____ and white flags waved from poles along

the woods. _____ little town _____ soon be

ready _____ visitors from the city. My friend and I were enjoying

the afternoon. The _____ of us rode our bikes along the dirt

_____ . A fisherman was tying his boat to the dock. He waved

to us.

"_____ have some good trout for _____ ,"

he shouted.

"_____ today, I called back.

Exploring Words and Word Parts: Review

Directions: Say the word that names each picture. Write the number of syllables that you hear in the box.

1.

$\square$

2.

$\square$

3.

$\square$

4.

$\square$

5.

$\square$

6.

$\square$

Directions: Use a slash (/) to divide each word into syllables.

7. s t r a w b e r r y   8. w a g o n   9. p l a y g r o u n d

10. r a t t l e   11. o c t o p u s   12. g i n g e r b r e a d

 CD-104291 • Jump Into Phonics • © Carson-Dellosa

NAME: _____   DATE: _____

End of Book Test

Directions: Say the name of each picture. Fill in the circle next to the letter of the beginning sound.

1.
   - ○ h
   - ○ t
   - ○ n

2.
   - ○ l
   - ○ m
   - ○ n

3.
   - ○ k
   - ○ t
   - ○ m

Directions: Say the name of each picture. Fill in the circle next to the letter of the middle sound.

4.
   - ○ p
   - ○ s
   - ○ d

5.
   - ○ r
   - ○ b
   - ○ t

6.
   - ○ w
   - ○ m
   - ○ d

Directions: Say the name of each picture. Fill in the circle next to the letter of the ending sound.

7.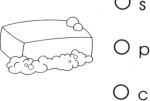
   - ○ s
   - ○ p
   - ○ c

8.
   - ○ n
   - ○ s
   - ○ t

9.
   - ○ b
   - ○ w
   - ○ d

End of Book Test, continued

Directions: Say the name of each picture. Fill in the circle next to the letters of the beginning sound.

10.
○ br
○ dr
○ fr
○ tr

11.
○ br
○ cr
○ fr
○ tr

12.
○ bl
○ cl
○ fl
○ sl

13.
○ bl
○ cl
○ fl
○ gl

14.
○ sc
○ sh
○ sp
○ st

15.
○ spr
○ str
○ scr
○ spl

Directions: Say the name of each picture. Fill in the circle next to the letters of the beginning sound.

16.
○ ch
○ sh
○ th
○ wh

17.
○ ch
○ sh
○ th
○ wh

18.
○ ch
○ sh
○ th
○ wh

Directions: Say the name of each picture. Fill in the circle next to the letters of the ending sound.

19.
○ ch
○ sh
○ th
○ wh

20.
○ ch
○ sh
○ th
○ wh

21.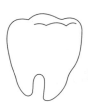
○ ch
○ sh
○ th
○ wh

CD-104291 • Jump Into Phonics • © Carson-Dellosa

End of Book Test, continued

Directions: Say the name of each picture. Fill in the circle next to the letter that is silent.

22.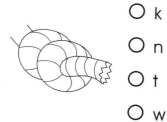
○ k
○ n
○ t
○ w

23.
○ c
○ n
○ r
○ w

24.
○ b
○ n
○ m
○ t

25.
○ g
○ s
○ t
○ w

26.
○ g
○ h
○ s
○ w

27.
○ g
○ l
○ s
○ t

Directions: Say the name of each picture. Fill in the circle next to the short vowel sound that you hear.

28.
○ ă
○ ĕ
○ ĭ
○ ŏ
○ ŭ

29.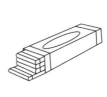
○ ă
○ ĕ
○ ĭ
○ ŏ
○ ŭ

30.
○ ă
○ ĕ
○ ĭ
○ ŏ
○ ŭ

31.
○ ă
○ ĕ
○ ĭ
○ ŏ
○ ŭ

32.
○ ă
○ ĕ
○ ĭ
○ ŏ
○ ŭ

33.
○ ă
○ ĕ
○ ĭ
○ ŏ
○ ŭ

End of Book Test, continued

Directions: Say the name of each picture. Fill in the circle next to the r-controlled vowel sound that you hear.

34.
○ ar
○ er
○ ir
○ or

35.
○ er
○ ir
○ or
○ ur

36.
○ er
○ ir
○ or
○ ur

37.
○ ar
○ er
○ ir
○ or

38.
○ ar
○ er
○ ir
○ or

39.
○ er
○ ir
○ or
○ ur

Directions: Say the name of each picture. Fill in the circle next to the long vowel sound that you hear.

40.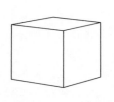
○ ā
○ ē
○ ī
○ ō
○ ū

41.
○ ā
○ ē
○ ī
○ ō
○ ū

42.
○ ā
○ ē
○ ī
○ ō
○ ū

43.
○ ā
○ ē
○ ī
○ ō
○ ū

44.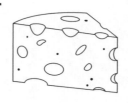
○ ā
○ ē
○ ī
○ ō
○ ū

45.
○ ā
○ ē
○ ī
○ ō
○ ū

CD-104291 • Jump Into Phonics • © Carson-Dellosa

End of Book Test, continued

Directions: Fill in the circle next to the vowel sound that the *y* makes in each word.

46. fly
    ○ ē
    ○ ī

47. city
    ○ ē
    ○ ī

48. study
    ○ ē
    ○ ī

Directions: Fill in the circle next to the word that names each picture.

49.
    ○ train
    ○ tray
    ○ tree
    ○ toast

50.
    ○ tray
    ○ say
    ○ hat
    ○ hay

51.
    ○ threw
    ○ thumb
    ○ three
    ○ think

52.
    ○ deer
    ○ bow
    ○ cow
    ○ boat

53.
    ○ sale
    ○ seen
    ○ deal
    ○ seal

54.
    ○ goat
    ○ boat
    ○ good
    ○ gold

55.
    ○ snow
    ○ seed
    ○ snail
    ○ trail

56.
    ○ goal
    ○ gold
    ○ gate
    ○ gale

57.
    ○ pen
    ○ bee
    ○ pea
    ○ pet

End of Book Test, continued

Directions: Fill in the circle next to the word that names each picture.

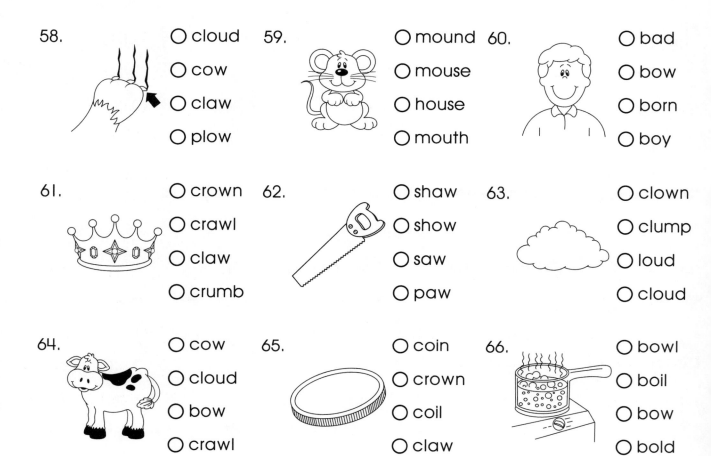

58.
- ○ cloud
- ○ cow
- ○ claw
- ○ plow

59.
- ○ mound
- ○ mouse
- ○ house
- ○ mouth

60.
- ○ bad
- ○ bow
- ○ born
- ○ boy

61.
- ○ crown
- ○ crawl
- ○ claw
- ○ crumb

62.
- ○ shaw
- ○ show
- ○ saw
- ○ paw

63.
- ○ clown
- ○ clump
- ○ loud
- ○ cloud

64.
- ○ cow
- ○ cloud
- ○ bow
- ○ crawl

65.
- ○ coin
- ○ crown
- ○ coil
- ○ claw

66.
- ○ bowl
- ○ boil
- ○ bow
- ○ bold

Directions: Fill in the circle next to the word that has the same *oo* vowel sound.

67.
- ○ tooth
- ○ wood
- ○ foot
- ○ book

68.
- ○ boot
- ○ igloo
- ○ book
- ○ moose

69.
- ○ cook
- ○ book
- ○ wood
- ○ igloo

End of Book Test, continued

Directions: Fill in the circle next to each word's prefix.

70. review
- ○ re
- ○ ew
- ○ rev
- ○ vi

71. unclear
- ○ un
- ○ ar
- ○ cl
- ○ nc

72. mislead
- ○ mis
- ○ ad
- ○ misl
- ○ lea

73. unable
- ○ le
- ○ bl
- ○ ble
- ○ un

74. rewrite
- ○ re
- ○ te
- ○ wr
- ○ it

75. misbehave
- ○ ve
- ○ mis
- ○ be
- ○ have

Directions: Fill in the circle next to each word's suffix.

76. biked
- ○ bi
- ○ ked
- ○ ed
- ○ bike

77. spinning
- ○ sp
- ○ ing
- ○ nn
- ○ g

78. teacher
- ○ t
- ○ ea
- ○ ch
- ○ er

79. talked
- ○ ta
- ○ lk
- ○ k
- ○ ed

80. glasses
- ○ gl
- ○ es
- ○ ss
- ○ s

81. farmer
- ○ f
- ○ ar
- ○ m
- ○ er

End of Book Test, continued

Directions: Fill in the circle next to the plural form of each word.

82. pig
- ○ piges
- ○ pigs
- ○ piggs
- ○ pigez

83. box
- ○ boxs
- ○ boxxes
- ○ boxes
- ○ boxess

84. branch
- ○ branches
- ○ branchs
- ○ branchess
- ○ branchez

85. leaf
- ○ leafs
- ○ leaves
- ○ leafes
- ○ leavess

86. bell
- ○ belles
- ○ bellses
- ○ bells
- ○ bellez

87. foot
- ○ feets
- ○ foots
- ○ footes
- ○ feet

88. dress
- ○ dressez
- ○ dresses
- ○ dress
- ○ dressees

89. brush
- ○ brushes
- ○ brushs
- ○ brushees
- ○ brushess

90. crown
- ○ crownes
- ○ crownss
- ○ crowness
- ○ crowns

91. child
- ○ childs
- ○ childes
- ○ children
- ○ childrens

92. toy
- ○ toys
- ○ toyez
- ○ toyes
- ○ toyss

93. mouse
- ○ mousess
- ○ mousez
- ○ mouses
- ○ mice

End of Book Test, continued

Directions: Fill in the circle next to the contraction for each word pair.

94. do not
  - ○ don't
  - ○ do'nt
  - ○ dont'
  - ○ do'not

95. they are
  - ○ theya're
  - ○ the'yre
  - ○ they're
  - ○ theyre'

96. he is
  - ○ he'is
  - ○ h'es
  - ○ he'ss
  - ○ he's

97. we will
  - ○ we'll
  - ○ wel'l
  - ○ we'wil
  - ○ we'ill

98. he would
  - ○ he'ld
  - ○ he'uld
  - ○ hed'
  - ○ he'd

99. should not
  - ○ should't
  - ○ shouldn't
  - ○ should'nt
  - ○ should'not

100. that is
  - ○ tha'ts
  - ○ that'is
  - ○ thats'
  - ○ that's

101. is not
  - ○ is'nt
  - ○ isnt'
  - ○ isn't
  - ○ is'not

102. it would
  - ○ it'd
  - ○ itd'
  - ○ itw'd
  - ○ i'tl

103. who will
  - ○ whow'll
  - ○ who'ill
  - ○ who'll
  - ○ wholl'

104. she has
  - ○ shes'
  - ○ she'as
  - ○ she'hs
  - ○ she's

105. have not
  - ○ haven't
  - ○ have'nt
  - ○ havenot'
  - ○ haventt'

End of Book Test, continued

Directions: Fill in the circle next to the number of syllables in each word.

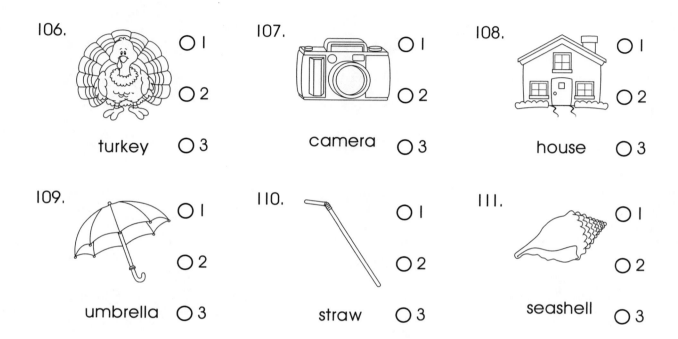

106. turkey
○ 1
○ 2
○ 3

107. camera
○ 1
○ 2
○ 3

108. house
○ 1
○ 2
○ 3

109. umbrella
○ 1
○ 2
○ 3

110. straw
○ 1
○ 2
○ 3

111. seashell
○ 1
○ 2
○ 3

Directions: Fill in the circle next to the correct way to divide each word into syllables.

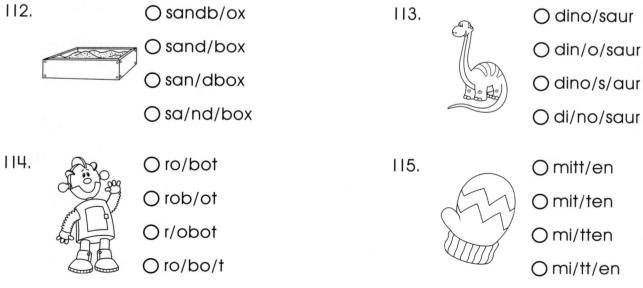

112.
○ sandb/ox
○ sand/box
○ san/dbox
○ sa/nd/box

113.
○ dino/saur
○ din/o/saur
○ dino/s/aur
○ di/no/saur

114.
○ ro/bot
○ rob/ot
○ r/obot
○ ro/bo/t

115.
○ mitt/en
○ mit/ten
○ mi/tten
○ mi/tt/en

End of Book Test, continued

Directions: Read each word. Fill in the circle next to the word that sounds the same.

116. flower
- ○ flier
- ○ flew
- ○ flour
- ○ flip

117. plane
- ○ plan
- ○ plain
- ○ plow
- ○ plant

118. deer
- ○ dare
- ○ door
- ○ dear
- ○ deep

Directions: Fill in the circle next to the word that completes each sentence.

119. Please _____ the window.
- ○ clothes
- ○ close

120. Have you _____ the book?
- ○ red
- ○ read

121. There are _____ cats.
- ○ four
- ○ for

122. The shirt was on _____ .
- ○ sale
- ○ sail

123. The _____ buzzed.
- ○ bee
- ○ be

124. Tom _____ a pony at camp.
- ○ rode
- ○ road

barking	bare	baby
blanket	bear	beach
branches	boxes	boat
celery	castle	brick

CD-104291 • Jump Into Phonics • © Carson-Dellosa

coin	clown	children
cube	crib	corn
dresses	don't	dinosaur
frog	fly	farmer

guitar	grapes	giraffe
knot	he's	hay
plant	paw	misplace
sauce	restart	pretzel

she'd	screw	scout
sleep	skirt	show
spider	snake	smile
star	spring	splash

tall	swing	stretches
they're	tallest	taller
tooth	took	thumb
tree	train	toy

CD-104291 • Jump Into Phonics • © Carson-Dellosa

waffles	unlike	unclear
whale	we've	wagon
yak	wrist	whistle
zebra	yo-yo	you'll

Answer Key

Pages 9–10

1. d; 2. m; 3. g; 4. f; 5. p; 6. s; 7. g; 8. r; 9. l; 10. t; 11. n; 12. k; 13. tt; 14. pp; 15. ll; 16. s; 17. k; 18. g; 19. j

Page 14

1. b; 2. l; 3. f; 4. c; 5. m; 6. d; 7. v; 8. b; 9. p

Page 15

1. j; 2. b; 3. c; 4. h; 5. f; 6. h; 7. c; 8. t; 9. t; 10. b; 11. v; 12. f

Page 16

1. c; 2. l; 3. m; 4. r; 5. g; 6. l; 7. y; 8. g; 9. d; 10. p; 11. n; 12. r

Page 17

1. nest, n; 2. hose, h; 3. pen, p; 4. log, l; 5. hook, h; 6. well, w; 7. dice, d; 8. car, c; 9. hat, h

Page 18

1. forest; 2. dog; 3. doll; 4. yard; 5. bat; 6. bed; 7. bib; 8. field

Page 19

1. b; 2. x; 3. g; 4. p; 5. t; 6. g; 7. p; 8. g; 9. b; 10. d; 11. r; 12. g

Page 20

cat: hot, jet, pet, rat; mop: cup, hop, rip, top

Page 21

1. rug; 2. bag; 3. pin; 4. cat; 5. yak; 6. leg; 7. map; 8. fan; 9. jar; 10. six; 11. bed; 12. ham

Page 22

1. n; 2. x; 3. t; 4. g; 5. k; 6. r; 7. cat, ball; 8. jam, bib; 9. van, gas

Page 23

x: ax, box, fox, six; l: bell, goal, well, shell

Page 24

1. ff; 2. rr; 3. mm; 4. gg; 5. tt; 6. bb; 7. tt; 8. pp

Page 25

mitten: glitter, kitten, button; hammer: summer, simmer; wallet: cellar, village, balloon; slippers: happen, pepper

Page 26

1. b; 2. v; 3. l, 4. m; 5. d

Page 27

1. g; 2. l; 3. w; 4. b; 5. v; 6. m; 7. t; 8. m; 9. x

Page 28

car: cake, cat, coat, cup; cent: celery, cell, circle, city

Page 29

1. hard c; 2. hard c; 3. soft c; 4. soft c; 5. hard c; 6. hard c; 7. soft c; 8. hard c; 9. hard c

Page 30

gum: game, gate, gold, guitar; giraffe: gem, germ, giant, gym

Page 31

1. hard g; 2. soft g; 3. hard g; 4. soft g; 5. hard g; 6. hard g; 7. hard g; 8. hard g; 9. hard g

Page 32

1. z; 2. l; 3. w; 4. d; 5. n; 6. l; 7. bb; 8. rr; 9. ff; 10. dd

CD-104291 • Jump Into Phonics • © Carson-Dellosa

Answer Key, continued

Page 33

1. bat, book; 2. penny, pear; 3. lemon, ladder; 4. balloon, mitten; 5. spider, guitar; 6. hat, boat; 7. river, cover; 8. kitten, kettle; 9. cabin, robin

Page 34

cake: car, cat; celery: cell, city; goat: gate, gold; giraffe: gem, giant

Pages 35–36

1. tr; 2. fl; 3. cl; 4. sm; 5. br; 6. sk; 7. whistle; 8. cheese; 9. shark; 10. leash; 11. fish; 12. fish, brush; 13. sandwich, bench; 14. k; 15. w; 16. c; 17. b

Page 40

1. branch; 2. bread; 3. brick; 4. brush; 5. trunk; 6. train; 7. truck; 8. tree

Page 41

1. dress; 2. drill; 3. drum; 4. dream; 5. drip; 6. draw; 7. draft; 8. drape

Page 42

1. crayon; 2. crib; 3. frame; 4. crab; 5. crown; 6. frog

Page 43

grapes: grass, gray, green, grin; pretzel: prince, print, prize, proud

Page 44

1. class; 2. glad; 3. gleam; 4. clap; 5. glance; 6. close

Page 45

block: blanket, blaze, blink, blue, bloom; plant: plaid, plan, plot, plow, plum

Page 46

1. fl; 2. fl; 3. sl; 4. sl; 5. fl; 6. sl; 7. sl; 8. fl; 9. fl

Page 47

1. scale; 2. skip; 3. sky; 4. scares; 5. skirt; 6. scout; 7. school; 8. skid

Page 48

smile: small, smart, smell, smooth; snail: snack, snake, snap, snow

Page 49

1. swing; 2. spool; 3. spoon; 4. swan; 5. spider; 6. sweater

Page 50

splash: splatter, splendid, splint, splinter, split, splurge; spring: sprawl, spray, spread, sprinkle, sprint, sprout

Page 51

screw: scrap, scream, scrape, scrub, screen; straw: string, stripe, street, strong, straight

Page 52

1; 2; 5; 6; 7; 9

Page 53

1; 3; 4; 5; 8

Page 54

1. ch; 2. sh; 3. sh; 4. sh; 5. sh; 6. ch; 7. ch; 8. ch; 9. ch

Page 55

2; 5; 6; 8

Page 56

tooth: both, math, moth, with; thimble: thorn, thirty, thumb, thermometer

Page 57

1. w; 2. k; 3. b; 4. b; 5. w; 6. t

Page 58

1. design; 2. chord; 3. castle; 4. sign; 5. whistle; 6. echo

Page 59

1. cl; 2. fr; 3. pl; 4. gl; 5. sl; 6. fl; 7. cr; 8. st; 9. dr

Page 60

1. cr; 2. gr; 3. fl; 4. br; 5. gl; 6. fr; 7. cl; 8. bl; 9. dr

Page 61

1. t; 2. w; 3. k; 4. k; 5. b; 6. t; 7. w; 8. k; 9. w

Page 62

1. whistle; 2. wheel; 3. shell; 4. shark; 5. thermometer; 6. cherry; 7. cheese; 8. chair; 9. thimble

Pages 63–64

1. ŭ; 2. ŏ; 3. ĭ; 4. ă; 5. ŏ; 6. ĕ; 7. ă; 8. ŭ; 9. ĕ; 10. ĭ; 11. log; 12. cat; 13. bus; 14. pen; 15. fish; 16. wig

Page 68

1; 2; 5; 7; 9

Page 69

1. bed; 2. jet; 3. pen; 4. bell; 5. ten; 6. net; 7. nest; 8. leg; 9. well

Page 70

hat: bag, bat, jam, tack; leg: bell, dress, nest, shell

Page 71

1. wig; 2. sit; 3. bib; 4. fin; 5. dig; 6. pig; 7. zip; 8. fish

Page 72

1. box; 2. mop; 3. fox; 4. top; 5. log; 6. rock; 7. frog; 8. doll; 9. clock; 10. block; 11. sock; 12. lock

Page 73

1; 3; 4; 5; 7; 9

Page 74

1. o; 2. u; 3. u; 4. o; 5. u; 6. o; 7. u; 8. o; 9. u

Page 75

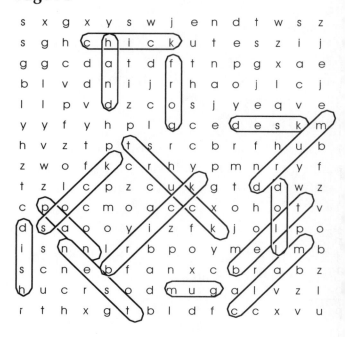

Page 76

1. e; 2. a; 3. e; 4. u; 5. u; 6. i; 7. e; 8. o; 9. i

Page 77

1. e; 2. e; 3. a; 4. u; 5. a; 6. i; 7. o; 8. u; 9. o

Page 78

1. star; 2. yarn; 3. jar; 4. shark; 5. barn; 6. car

Page 79

1. fern; 2. girl; 3. bird; 4. turtle; 5. thirty; 6. nurse

Page 80

1. corn; 2. horse; 3. horn; 4. fork; 5. door; 6. thorn

Page 81

1. ŏ; 2. ă; 3. ĕ; 4. ŭ; 5. ă; 6. ŏ; 7. ĭ; 8. ĕ; 9. ŭ; 10. ĭ; 11. thorn, yarn, perch, star, fern, turtle, story, girl, thirty

Answer Key, continued

Page 82

1. ŏ; 2. ĭ; 3. ĕ; 4. o; 5. a; 6. u; 7. e; 8. i; 9. u

Page 83

pear: bear, chair; corn: born, horn; bird: surf, nurse, stir, fern; star: barn, park

Page 84

1. ā; 2. ī; 3. ē; 4. ō; 5. ū; 6. ī; 7. ē; 8. ō; 9. ā; 10. tape; 11. fire; 12. fire; 13. tape; 14. bone; 15. key; 16. unicycle; 17. unicycle; 18. key; 19. bone

Page 89

1. rain; 2. ape; 3. train; 4. snake; 5. table; 6. play; 7. mane; 8. grade; 9. plate; 10. bake

Page 90

acorn: apron, cage, cake, paint, rake; fan: bag, bat, candle, hat, map

Page 91

1; 3; 4; 7; 8

Page 92

tree: bean, green, queen, sheet, sleep; leg: desk, nest, step, tent, test

Page 93

1. kite; 2. vine; 3. tire; 4. bike; 5. smile; 6. ripe; 7. prize; 8. time; 9. mice; 10. light

Page 94

1; 5; 6; 7; 8; 9; 10; 12

Page 95

1; 5; 6; 7; 8; 10; 12

Page 96

boat: float, hope, joke, note, road; fox: box, clock, dog, doll, top

Page 97

1. unicycle; 2. uniform; 3. unit; 4. museum; 5. music; 6. humor; 7. ukelele; 8. menu; 9. tube; 10. juice

Page 98

1; 2; 4; 6; 9

Page 99

1. early; 2. sky; 3. puppy; 4. dry; 5. study; 6. family

Page 100

fly: cry, dry, eye, my, sky; baby: city, early, happy, story, study

Page 101

cage: acorn, face; tree: zebra, easy, sneeze; kite: spider, bike; nose: bone, robe; unicycle: cube, music

Page 102

1. ē; 2. ā; 3. ō; 4. ū; 5. ī; 6. ē; 7. ā; 8. ō; 9. ī

Page 103

cake: apron, table; bee: key, steep; lion: ripe, slide; rope: broke, grow; unicycle: uniform, unit

Pages 104–105

1. boy; 2. owl; 3. house; 4. crown; 5. boil; 6. cloud; 7. snail; 8. play; 9. beach; 10. knee; 11. pause; 12. float; 13. grow; 14. saw

Page 109

1. tail; 2. sail; 3. chain; 4. rain; 5. paint; 6. braid; 7. train; 8. snail; 9. nail

Page 110

eat, each, leaf, meat, tea, sea

Page 111

1. bee; 2. wheel; 3. three; 4. queen; 5. feet; 6. deer; 7. cheese; 8. tree; 9. seed

Page 112

1. beach; 2. team; 3. seal; 4. dream; 5. treat;
6. cream; 7. stream; 8. beam

Page 113

boat, coach, coat, float, foam, goal, toast

Page 114

1. bow; 2. know; 3. blow; 4. grow; 5. flow;
6. slow; 7. tow; 8. low

Page 115

snail: nail, paint, rain, tail, train; tree: bee, deer,
knee, sheep, wheel

Page 116

clay, pay, tray, play, way, maybe

Page 117

pea: bead, beam, clean, teach, team;
bow: blow, crow, grow, know, sow

Page 118

1; 3; 5; 7; 8; 9

Page 119

1; 3; 4; 5; 7; 8

Page 120

haul, launch, yawn, claw, pause, draw, fawn

Page 121

book: foot, cookie, hook, look, cook;
moon: igloo, boot, tooth, spoon, roof

Page 122

1. nail; 2. wheel; 3. bow; 4. boat; 5. seal;
6. hay; 7. train, brain; 8. queen, bee;
9. boat, toast

Page 123

1. boil, soy; 2. foil, joy; 3. mouse, frown;
4. house, clown; 5. claw, sauce; 6. launch,
yawn

Page 124

1. rain; 2. hay; 3. tree; 4. team; 5. toast;
6. show

Pages 125–126

1. re; 2. mis; 3. un; 4. mis; 5. un; 6. re; 7. un;
8. re; 9. mis; 10. ed; 11. est; 12. ing; 13. s;
14. er; 15. es; 16. s; 17. est; 18. ed; 19. b;
20. e; 21. g; 22. d; 23. a; 24. f; 25. c

Page 130

1. reread; 2. replay; 3. rewrite; 4. reheat;
5. reheat; 6. reread; 7. rewrite; 8. replay

Page 131

1. unsure, not sure; 2. unclear, not clear;
3. unwell, not well; 4. unable, not able;
5. unknown, not known; 6. unlike, not alike;
7. unhappy, not happy; 8. unfriendly, not
friendly; 9. unafraid, not afraid; 10. unfair,
not fair

Page 132

1. mislead; 2. misbehave; 3. misplace;
4. misspell; 5. misbehave; 6. misspell;
7. misplace; 8. mislead

Page 133

Answers will vary but may include: 1. redone,
do again; 2. reuse, use again; 3. recall, call
again; 4. unlike, not like; 5. misjudge, judge
incorrectly; 6. recharge, charge again;
7. remake, make again; 8. recount, count
again; 9. replay, play again; 10. recover,
cover again

Page 134

1. biked; 2. raced; 3. laced; 4. raked; 5. liked;
6. baked; 7. joked; 8. promised

Page 135

1. running; 2. popping; 3. batting; 4. spinning;
5. running; 6. spinning; 7. batting; 8. popping

Page 136

1. barking; 2. walking; 3. reading; 4. building;
5. barking; 6. building; 7. reading; 8. walking

Page 137

1. speaker; 2. singer; 3. farmer; 4. player;
5. player; 6. farmer; 7. singer; 8. speaker

Page 138

1. taller; 2. oldest; 3. bigger; 4. funniest;
5. neater; 6. happiest; 7. harder; 8. tallest

Page 139

1. dogs; 2. hats; 3. bells; 4. frogs; 5. pigs;
6. mugs

Page 140

1. foxes; 2. dresses; 3. branches; 4. peaches;
5. boxes; 6. brushes

Page 141

1. hatches; 2. works; 3. plays; 4. catches;
5. helps; 6. stretches

Page 142

1. dice; 2. oxen; 3. children; 4. teeth; 5. feet;
6. men

Page 143

1. d; 2. b; 3. f; 4. e; 5. c; 6. a; 7. faster;
8. wisest; 9. tallest; 10. louder

Page 144

1. mice; 2. banana; 3. book; 4. dress; 5. bees;
6. oxen; 7. pie; 8. boxes; 9. spoon

Page 145

1. restart; 2. cats; 3. unsure; 4. oldest;
5. banker; 6. misplace

Pages 146–149

1. didn't; 2. here's; 3. you'll; 4. she'd; 5. you're;
6. he'd; 7. she's; 8. you'd; 9. they're; 10. we're;
11. we'll; 12. they'd; 13. pen/cil; 14. rab/bit;
15. skate/board; 16. ro/bot; 17. night, knight
(no); 18. flour, flower (yes); 19. blue, blew (no);
20. weak, week (yes); 21. bear; 22. eye;
23. ant; 24. eight; 25. flower; 26. pear;
27. 2; 28. 2; 29. 3; 30. 1; 31. 2; 32. 3; 33. 2;
34. 1; 35. mo/tor; 36. pan/cake; 37. bi/cycle;
38. cam/el; 39. oc/to/pus; 40. pil/low;
41. pic/nic; 42. base/ball; 43. di/no/saur;
44. straw/ber/ry

Page 155

1. haven't; 2. isn't; 3. hadn't; 4. can't;
5. haven't; 6. didn't; 7. hasn't; 8. don't

Page 156

1. aren't; 2. can't; 3. couldn't; 4. didn't ;
5. doesn't; 6. don't; 7. hadn't; 8. hasn't; 9. isn't;
10. wasn't; 11. haven't; 12. weren't

Page 157

1. I'll; 2. you'll; 3. He'll; 4. They'll; 5. she'll;
6. we'll

Page 158

1. They've; 2. She's; 3. You've; 4. I've; 5. He's;
6. We've

Page 159

1. She's; 2. it's; 3. Here's; 4. Who's; 5. What's;
6. that's

Page 160

1. we're; 2. They're; 3. You're; 4. They're;
5. we're; 6. you're

Page 161

1. We'd; 2. she'd; 3. they'd; 4. you'd; 5. he'd;
6. it'd

Page 162

1. I'd; 2. he'd; 3. they'd; 4. it'd; 5. she'd;
6. we'd; 7. you'd; 8. that'd; 9. she'd; 10. it'd;
11. they'd; 12. he'd

Page 163

1. I'll; 2. you'd; 3. he'd; 4. isn't; 5. they've;
6. we're; 7. she's; 8. hasn't; 9. that'd; 10. it's;
11. couldn't; 12. we'll; 13. he's; 14. couldn't;
15. I'm

Page 164

1. e; 2. h; 3. a; 4. c; 5. j; 6. b; 7. d; 8. i; 9. f;
10. g

Page 165

1. It's; 2. We'll; 3. don't; 4. he'd; 5. isn't; 6.
aren't; 7. she'll; 8. they're; 9. Don't; 10. We're

Page 166

1. not; 2. is; 3. not; 4. are; 5. will; 6. have;
7. not; 8. is; 9. would; 10. will

Page 167

1. 2; 2. 1; 3. 3; 4. 3; 5. 2; 6. 2; 7. 2; 8. 1; 9. 2

Page 168

1. nap/kin; 2. but/ter; 3. win/dow; 4. mit/ten;
5. yel/low; 6. pic/nic; 7. doc/tor; 8. let/ter;
9. tar/get; 10. pil/low; 11. pep/per; 12. pen/cil;
13. cen/ter; 14. car/rot; 15. zip/per

Page 169

1. cab/in; 2. ho/tel; 3. mo/tor; 4. ti/ger;
5. pu/pil; 6. shiv/er; 7. wa/ter; 8. fla/vor;
9. o/pen; 10. shov/el; 11. pi/lot; 12. re/port;
13. i/tem; 14. mon/ey

Page 170

1. snow/man; 2. wind/mill; 3. bath/tub;
4. note/book; 5. sea/shell; 6. rain/bow

Page 171

1. bi/cy/cle; 2. di/no/saur; 3. sun/glas/ses;
4. to/ma/to; 5. news/pa/per; 6. la/dy/bug;
7. el/e/phant; 8. pi/a/no; 9. um/brel/la

Page 172

1. din/ner; 2. com/pu/ter; 3. pock/et;
4. tel/e/phone; 5. pen/cil; 6. fa/mous;
7. sand/box; 8. crick/et; 9. but/ter/fly;
10. cam/el; 11. al/pha/bet; 12. ro/bot

Page 173

1. ham/mer; 2. kan/ga/roo; 3. cray/on;
4. ear/muffs; 5. pump/kin; 6. bal/loon; 7. tur/tle;
8. di/no/saur; 9. lad/der

Page 174

Answers will vary.

Page 175

1. i; 2. f; 3. j; 4. k; 5. a; 6. b; 7. a; 8. l; 9. e;
10. c; 11. g; 12. h

Page 176

1. be; 2. bee; 3. two; 4. to; 5. blew; 6. blue;
7. red; 8. read

Page 177

1. I; 2. eye; 3. close; 4. clothes; 5. four; 6. for;
7. bare; 8. bear

Page 178

1. f; 2. d; 3. a; 4. h; 5. b; 6. c; 7. j; 8. e; 9. g;
10. i

Page 179

1. I'm; 2. they'll; 3. she's; 4. It's; 5. we'll;
6. You're; 7. wasn't; 8. he'll; 9. doesn't

Page 180

1. f; 2. d; 3. a; 4. j; 5. b; 6. i; 7. c; 8. g; 9. e;
10. h